# PIETIST AND WESLEYAN STUDIES

**Editors: David Bundy and J. Steven O'Malley**

This monograph series will publish volumes in two areas of scholarly research: Pietism and Methodism (broadly understood). The focus will be Pietism, its history and development, and the influence of this socioreligious tradition in modern culture, especially within the Wesleyan religious traditions.

Consideration will be given to scholarly works on classical and neo-Pietism, on English and American Methodism, as well as on the social and ecclesiastical institutions shaped by Pietism (e.g., Evangelicals, United Brethren, and the Pietist traditions among the Lutherans, Reformed, and Anabaptists). Works focusing on leaders within the Pietist and Wesleyan traditions will also be included in the series, as well as occasional translations and/or editions of Pietist texts. It is anticipated that the monographs will emphasize theological developments, but with close attention to the interaction of Pietism with other cultural forces and to the sociocultural identity of the Pietist and Wesleyan movements.

1. Gregory S. Clapper, *John Wesley on Religious Affections.* 1989.
2. Peter Erb, *Gottfried Arnold.* 1989.

# JOHN WESLEY ON RELIGIOUS AFFECTIONS:

## his views on experience and emotion and their role in the Christian life and theology

by
GREGORY S. CLAPPER

with an Introduction by
Don E. Saliers

*Pietist and Wesleyan Studies, No. 1*

*The Scarecrow Press, Inc.*
*Metuchen, N.J., & London*
*1989*

The author gratefully acknowledges the following for granting permission to reprint their materials:

Abingdon Press for excerpts from *The Works of John Wesley*, Vol. 4, edited by Albert Outler. Copyright ℗ 1987 by Abingdon Press. Used by permission.

Epworth Press for excerpts from *Explanatory Notes Upon the New Testament*, by John Wesley. Reprinted by Epworth Press, 1976.

British Library Cataloguing-in-Publication data available

Library of Congress Cataloging-in-Publication Data

Clapper, Gregory Scott.
    John Wesley on religious affections : his views on experience and emotion and their role in Christian life and theology / by Gregory S. Clapper ; with an introduction by Don E. Saliers.
        p.   cm. --(Pietist and Wesleyan studies ; no. 1)
    Revision of thesis (Ph.D.)--Emory University, 1985.
    Includes bibliographical references.
    ISBN 0-8108-2267-9 (alk. paper)
    1. Wesley, John, 1703-1791--Contributions in doctrine of religious affections.   2. Experience (Religion)--History of doctrines --18th century.   3. Emotions--Religious aspects--Christianity--History of doctrines--18th century.   I. Title.   II. Series.
BR110.C53   1989                                 89-39661
248.2--dc20

Copyright ℗ 1989 by Gregory S. Clapper

Manufactured in the United States of America

Printed on acid-free paper

For Jody

# EDITORS' FOREWORD

The current resurgence of interest in John Wesley as a source for contemporary theological reflection, coincident with the bibliographical work of Frank Baker and the development of the Oxford-Abingdon edition of Wesley's works, has produced a number of dissertations and studies. Much of that work has focused on classical theological and historical concerns, all of which are important and have their scholarly validity. Only recently has scholarly attention been turned toward the "piety" or "spirituality" of the founder of the Methodist traditions.

Wesley is a problematic subject of study. His work was forged in the process of a decades-long peripatetic ministry, usually removed from the centers of British intellectual life. Because of the genre of his theological reflection (sermons, journals, letters, tracts, editions of religious texts, scholia on scripture), it has become a truism of the academy that Wesley (and by logical connection, Methodism) was deficient in his theological foundations. That conclusion is now being successfully challenged.

It is the goal of the series, Pietist and Wesleyan Studies, to contribute to the project of revision by exploring the relations between Wesley and Wesleyan spirituality and the theological and ministerial structures of the Wesleyan tradition. Gregory Clapper's study of Wesley's views on experience and emotion and on their role in Christian life and theology inaugurates the Wesley section of the series.

Following undergraduate studies at Carthage College (B.A. 1974), Gregory Clapper pursued graduate study in philosophy at the University of Wisconsin--Milwaukee

(M.A. 1977) and in theology at Garrett-Evangelical Theological Seminary (M.Div. 1979). He undertook his doctoral studies at Emory University in theology (Ph.D. 1985). Clapper is Associate Professor of Religion and Philosophy at Westmar College.

We are pleased to publish his study as the first volume of Pietist and Wesleyan Studies.

David Bundy
Associate Professor of
   Christian Origins
Collection Development
   Librarian
Asbury Theological
   Seminary
Wilmore, KY

J. Stephen O'Malley
Professor of
   Church History
   and Historical
   Theology
Asbury Theological
   Seminary
Wilmore, KY

# JOHN WESLEY ON RELIGIOUS AFFECTIONS:
His Views on Experience and Emotion and Their Role in
the Christian Life and Theology

## Table of Contents

**Chapter Four,** Continued:

# PREFACE

This work is a revision of my Ph.D. dissertation which was originally accepted by the Department of Theological Studies of Emory University. The re-writing began while I served as Visiting Professor of Theology at the Metodistkirkens Studiesenter in Bergen, Norway. I am thankful for the support given to me by both the Studie-senter and my home school of Westmar College. I am honored that this work will appear in the Pietist and Wesleyan Studies Series.

My interest in the nature of emotion and its implications for theology began when I was an undergraduate studying both philosophy (where emotion was often ignored) and psychology (where it was often deified). In graduate school, reading works by people like Wittgenstein, Augustine, Edwards, Schleiermacher, Kierkegaard, and Scheler, I started to see that neither of the above extreme approaches does full justice to the subtlety of "emotional" reality. This present work on Wesley's thought came about when I discovered that Wesley's conception of the "religious affections" was quite sophisticated and could stand up well to a critique of both modern theorists of emotion and "post-modern" theologians. Indeed, I am convinced that Wesley has something important to say to the contemporary theological community concerning the fundamentally relational nature of Christian emotion. It is my hope that my exposition of Wesley's views will allow the reader to judge for her- or himself.

The Jackson edition of Wesley's *Works*, Telford's *Letters*, and Curnock's *Journal* were all consulted during my researches, though I have tried to reference most citations to the new Abingdon Press *Works* series. I thank Abingdon for permission to quote from this series. Portions of chapter six were originally published in *Wesleyan Theology Today* and in the *Wesleyan Theological Journal* and portions of chapter seven first appeared in *The Christian Century* (see bibliography for references).

Gratitude being one of the more important religious affections, I want to express mine to several people important to me. Dr. Don E. Saliers served as my adviser on the dissertation and I thank him for all that he has taught me, academically, but also on a more personal level. Special thanks go to Dr. Albert C. Outler, who first suggested that I look into Wesley's views concerning the affections, as well as to Dr. Frank Baker and his wife, Nellie, who showed me much kindness during my research for this work. Also greatly appreciated was access to the files of Rex Matthews, which contained many articles on the thought of John Wesley. The encouragement and very helpful comments of Tom Albin are also gladly noted. Dr. Garnett Wilder and the North Georgia Annual Conference of the United Methodist Church have been very supportive of me and my ministry and for that I am grateful.

My Ph.D. studies were made possible by a grant from A Foundation for Theological Education for which I remain deeply grateful. I am also grateful for the generous support of my mother and my wife during the writing and revision of this work. My wife, Jody, has given me more than I could ever thank her for. Let my dedication of this work to her be one sign of my gratitude for all of her gifts.

I thank Paul Carlson for showing me, when I needed to see it, that not everything in life is a cynical joke. My thanks also go to Paul Hessert, Thomas Flynn, Ted Runyon, Jack Boozer and William Mallard, all of whom have helped form my understanding of what Christianity is about. I thank my daughters, Laura and Jenna, for being who they are, and I thank God from Whom all blessings flow.

# INTRODUCTION

**Don E. Saliers, Emory University**

We should not be surprised that clichés and caricatures abound when it comes to the life and writings of John Wesley. To those concerned with systematic theology, he presents a hopelessly unsystematic literature--sermons, midrash on Scripture he calls *Notes*, abridged and selectively edited treatises, not to mention journals, diaries and letters. To those concerned with doctrinal propositions or with social-ethical foundations, he appears uncritically preoccupied with inner piety. Gregory Clapper observes that in Wesley's own time, "To the enthusiast, he sounded like a rationalist. To the rationalist, he sounded like an enthusiast. To the quietist caught up in the 'inner' life, he would...sound like an activist." (p. 172) Precisely because Wesley took aim at specific misunderstandings of doctrine, piety and practice, shaping arguments and evidence to correct these in specific contexts, the problem of caricature intensifies. This was so in the eighteenth century, and often remains so today.

One of the virtues of this study is its refusal to be misled by Wesley's multiple strategies and by the unsystematic, seemingly *ad hoc* occasioning of his theological thinking. In tracing how Wesley reasons about the nature and role of religious affections in Scripture, in homiletical material, by his reflection on the life-issues of the Christian community, and in his approach to Jonathan Edwards' *Treatise*, the author makes a case for what we may call the "systemic" rather than the systematic Wesley: he illuminates Wesley's synoptic view of the interrelatedness of doctrine and experience, of reason and emotion. Wesley's strategies to address various misunderstandings are finally grounded in his core convictions about the initiating, sustaining and consummating grace of God in Christ; but those strategies attend robustly to human consciousness, intention, and action. This, in part, accounts for Wesley's abridgement of Edwards, for any doctrine that seemed to deny human freedom in relation to God's free offer of grace sounded to Wesley to be contrary to the Gospel. It is another matter, of course, to claim that Wesley's reading of Edwards and of the Calvinist tradition was fully adequate or fair.

Three significant strands in Clapper's approach to Wesley deserve further mention at the outset. First, Wesley does in fact have a contribution to make to the analysis and clarification of religious experience. Attention to the "logic" of emotions which has developed in recent twentieth century philosophical psychology is compatible with Wesley's non-theoretical manner of thinking about, as well as thinking with, the religious affections. We see this most clearly in chapters Four and Seven. Clapper's term, *orthokardia*, is a summary concept which signifies this side of Wesley's work. Wesley is certainly concerned with "heart-religion", but precisely in a manner which can speak of thought as integral to having emotions, and furthermore of emotional dispositions in the believer as being ingredient in rendering right judgments about God and the world. How this style of thinking in Wesley differs from Schleiermacher's account of the religious affections is a comparative question invited by the contrast of "orthokardia" with orthodoxy and orthopraxy. In elaborating this orthokardia, Clapper shows how Wesley's understanding of the contingent nature of religious affectivity is more illuminating than Schleiermacher's emphasis on a universal and innate "feeling".

A second strand of Clapper's study highlights the multiple literary forms employed by Wesley. His literature is indeed a rich polyglot, and certainly not systematic or speculative. Yet we are invited to consider how a unified sense of the graced pattern of life, at once communal and interior, grounded in what God has done in Christ, requires a multi-faceted literature in order to do justice to its reality. Clapper urges us to see this continuity in Wesley, challenging us to read more carefully.

Finally, this study invites a fresh reading of Wesley as a practical theologian. In one sense the whole study shows all of Wesley's writings to be a series of concrete specifications of the "grammar" of the Christian life. The move from Wesley's *Notes* on both Testaments through his sermons and the abridged *Treatise* manifests a unitive vision despite the circumstantial nature of Wesley's attention. Here we may read with the author to determine the extent to which Wesley's account of the religious affections is fundamentally *relational* rather than merely psychological or "emotive." We may then be in a better position to assess the tensions that remain between "inner" and "outer" holiness that other commentators on Wesley find to be ambiguities. We may instead find that these tensions are the unintended but necessary result of Wesley's vigorous practical dialogue with a variety of misunderstandings of the role of experience in the Christian life.

# CHAPTER ONE

## An Introduction to
## the "Religious Affections" and "Experience"
## and the Critical Questions That They Raise

The "emotions" are a crucial part of human existence, some would even say they are the defining aspect of a human life. Because of this, theology - the Church's reflections on God and humanity - must, in every generation, come to grips with affectivity. Theology must understand the causes, the nature, and the importance of felt experience within the religious life. The range of possible positions on these issues is quite broad.

Some say the emotions are "secondary qualities," akin to how some philosophers used to regard the phenomenon of color, i.e., something which merely enlivens the structures of reality which are independently established by "reason." Others have asserted that the theologian should say, with Hume, that reason must be the servant of the passions. In any case, those who take the Biblical witness seriously must decide: Is the great range of scriptural language about the "heart" dispensable ornamentation which only clouds the real message of the Gospel, or does this emotion-language itself convey and constitute, in large measure, the real message?

A key problem confronting any theologian who wishes to sort out these issues is that many thinkers in the Western tradition have ignored the broad questions that emotion raises for theology.[1] One important exception to this generalization is John Wesley. In his sermons, essays,

1

Biblical commentaries and various abridgements, Wesley has given us some definitive insights regarding the importance of emotion for Christianity.

## "Experience" and the Affections in Wesley's Thought

"Experience" has long been taken to be a distinctive emphasis of Wesley's theology. The United Methodist Church, the largest organizational heir to Wesley's legacy, has officially pronounced the so-called "quadrilateral" of Scripture, tradition, experience and reason to be the "four main sources and guidelines for Christian theology."[2] In trying to understand these terms, "experience" often proves to be the most elusive. Some take it to mean merely that individuals must personally appropriate the truth of Christianity, while others have taken experience by itself to be an actual source of doctrine. Neither of these options correctly depict Wesley's full understanding of the term.

The major problem with defining Wesley's views on "experience" is that while his theology is what we might call an "experiential" theology, the term "experience" was used by Wesley in his religious discourse in a general way, as a kind of gathering term which encompassed many kinds of different, individual experiences. To see what was at stake in his various claims about "experience" we have to refer to concrete experiences which typically found expression in the language of emotion. This emotion or affection language (what we may call the basic or first-order language, the idiom of common discourse) was Wesley's primary mode of expression. He spoke about the various contexts and different kinds of love, joy, fear, peace, etc., when he was pushed by circumstances to explain what he meant by the over-arching and more theoretical term "experience."

While Wesley was well educated and knew the technical discourse of philosophers and classical theologians, he consciously eschewed these intellectually fashionable vocabularies in his preaching and writing which he addressed to the common listener. This is one of the reasons he is justly considered a "folk" theologian rather than a classical systematician. However, we should not let such a characterization prejudice us against Wesley, for there is much more at stake here than a point of rhetorical strategy.

If, as I will show Wesley believed, being a Christian consists, to a large extent, of having certain religious affections, then Wesley's affection-laden language is not a pandering to the masses but is in fact the most true and adequate way to talk about Christianity. This language is, therefore, a direct expression of his theological (not merely rhetorical) grasp of the Christian faith. In order best to understand the experiential elements of his theology, we must look to his depiction of the religious affections.

## The Context of This Study

### The Present Need for a Truly Practical Theology

In every age, theological temptations abound. There is no way that Gnosticism or Pelagianism can ever be dealt with once and for all; there is no way of totally eradicating Sabellianism or Donatism even if this were deemed desirable. Certain conceptions will always offer themselves as more attractive alternatives to the faith of the received tradition.

One concept which consistently fosters confusions, misunderstandings and mistakes is that of "religious experience." Whether it is called "emotionalism," "pietism," "enthusiasm" or even "mysticism," an over-emphasis on "experience" in the Christian life has always arisen in, and been proscribed by, the Western philosophical and theological traditions. What is less often recognized, though, is that certain affections *do* have a normative role to play in the Christian life, and that to deny this is just as wrong as over-emphasizing it.

Many forms of worship and celebration in use today, for example, still emphasize the affective life[3], but current theology has been more concerned with methodology and socio-economics than with the felt experience of the believer. One manifestation of this current theological neglect of the affections can be seen in the typical seminary curriculum.

"How does that feel?" is probably one of the most repeated phrases in any contemporary seminary community, to say nothing of the therapeutic community at large. Theological schools have become enamored with things internal because they aim at training women and men to go out into the crying, laughing, despairing and rejoicing world and proclaim the Good News. Humanity is not seen as a collection of cold logicians whose only desire is to hear and stoically acknowledge adequately verifiable true propositions. Humanity is seen by the church to be God's good creation which groans after its Lord and weeps and gnashes its teeth without Him. A bare intellectual grasp of doctrine didactically conveyed will only fall on ears which have been deafened by the emotional roar of lived experience.

Unfortunately, all too often in the seminary the concern for affective realities is expressed only in the context of pastoral counseling. This discipline, the latter-day successor to the liturgical rites of confession and repentance, draws heavily upon the insights of contemporary psychology and only occasionally incorporates elements of the time-honored tradition of spiritual direction. The specifically theological content present in this mix, therefore, varies greatly between the many schools of thought and among the multitude of individual practitioners.

One implication of this curricular departmentalization of the affections is that the normative thrust of theology (which asks the question "What is Christianity all about?") is usually carried on without reference to the meat and potatoes of existence - the emotional life. Conversely, the "practical" courses of the seminary curriculum rush with relish to the hearty fare of affectivity, but, all too often, they do so without the utensils which can make the feast digestible - an adequately thought-through appropriation of the Gospel.

There have been several recent popular theological orientations which have tried to reconcile intellectual adequacy with emotional reality in a Christian way. The most notable of these, the existentialist school of Bultmann and Tillich, *et al.*, has been criticized by neo-orthodoxy as merely giving Christian names to the peaks and valleys of human experience instead of proclaiming the Christian landscape. Similarly, movements as diverse as process theology, pop psychology and the theology of success emphasize the non-cognitive aspects of life, but these views have also been criticized (often justifiably) for failing to assimilate the peculiarly Christian story into their systems.

Can the theology of John Wesley offer a viable alternative to this dilemma of the contemporary context? Does Wesley's theological orientation do justice to both the life of the heart and the heart of the Gospel? Can a late-twentieth century vision of human life and the Gospel be reconciled with a vision from the eighteenth century?

It is clear, even to those with only a cursory knowledge of his thought, that, indeed, for Wesley, the emotions are of crucial importance for the Christian life. This emphasis may appear, though, on the face of it, already to remove Wesley from serious modern consideration. Emphasizing the affections seems to plant Wesley squarely in the pious ooze of an era best forgotten. But we need to be patient and understand both the nature of emotion and also Wesley's views about it (not our prejudiced caricatures of his views) before we judge him so harshly.

Emotions, in Wesley's time as well as now, are a large and undeniable component of what it means to live a concrete, earthly existence, and, as Theodore Runyon has pointed out in a different context, Wesley made "concrete truth more ultimate than theories that do not affect life."[4] It is this desire to stay close to concrete reality that made Wesley think long and hard about the relation between felt experience and Christian truth. It is the need for a vision of the Gospel which is fully integrated with the very real and concrete life of the heart (evidenced by the booming growth in the field known as "Practical Theology") which should make us at least give another hearing to the theology of John Wesley.

### Contemporary Challenges to "Heart Religion"

What are "religious affections"? This question will be answered inductively through the course of the study, allowing Wesley's full understanding of the affections to unfold as we proceed, instead of giving a definition in advance. To begin, let us simply understand the phrase "religious affections" in a non-technical way, emphasizing the cognitive content of its component words. Even if the expression sounds a little quaint to twentieth century ears, the idea of emotions which are somehow related to religious beliefs is still conveyed by it. That is enough of an understanding to get us under way.

Aside from the basic question of what religious affections are, there are several other questions - critical, if not accusing, questions - which arise when "inner" experience is discussed in a contemporary religious context. Some of these questions are:

* Does speaking about the religious affections commit us to irrationality? Is not anything emotional necessarily irrational?

* Does an emphasis on the religious affections in the Christian life leave us blind to the problem of self-deception? Have not Freud and others shown us that all that comes from "inside" of us is nothing but the urge for base need fulfillment, often disguised by a thin patina of more socially acceptable intentions and desires?

* If the affectional life is of central importance to Christianity, does this mean it is a religion of self-absorption or spiritual narcissism which deems the social dimension of life unimportant? Is Wesley making the achievement of certain inner feeling-states the end or goal of Christianity?

The reader should detect a philosopher guarding against the fideist in the first question, a psychologist guarding against the fanatic in the second and a Marxist or liberationist guarding against the quietist in the third. This is the intellectual climate which exists today and these are the questions which must be heard and answered. The concerns expressed in these questions have motivated, formed and guided the present study and answers to them will be made apparent in the course of the exposition. The pervading influence of these questions reveals my work to be primarily theological rather than historical.[5]

The twentieth century has seen the development of a sizable body of literature concerning the nature of emotion,[6] and many of the insights found in this literature have already been appropriated and expressed by theologians.[7] Among these insights are the fact that an emotion can be differentiated from feeling states, that emotions can be seen as dispositions to behave, and that emotions, by and large, take objects, i.e., they arise by targeting certain aspects of reality.[8] These insights are also part of the context of my study and I will explain and use these conceptual tools in the course of my analysis of Wesley's views on the affections.

With these questions and conceptual tools in hand, then, we will engage Wesley's publications in order to understand his conception of the religious affections. We will not be primarily concerned with how well Wesley himself could evoke or evince any particular emotions, i.e., we will not be concerned with judging his effectiveness as a rhetorician, orator or liturgist. The goal is to capture Wesley's conceptual, theological reflections about the role of emotion in the Christian life in order to arrive at a critically constructive view which is relevant to our present-day theological concerns.

## The Scope of This Study

According to David Kelsey, theologians attempt to articulate and present their visions of Christianity.[9] Rather than an argument or an attempt at some kind of proof, the theologian's writings, taken as a whole, are an attempt to say what Christianity is - they are a proclamation, a witness. Central to Wesley's vision of Christianity was that a "great part of true religion lies in the affections"[10] and it is my goal in this study to spell out what Wesley did and did not mean by this.

Recent reflection which has focused specifically on the affective element of religion has usually had one of three goals. Such writing has aimed at establishing either

> 1) that a certain religious tradition can be known to be universally true if certain experiences occur (i.e.

that there are such things as self-validating religious experiences[11]), or

2) that any religion will contain certain affective elements (i.e. that there are a certain number of archetypal forms of "mysticism" or "religious experience"[12]), or

3) that Christianity necessarily contains certain patterns of affectivity.[13]

Wesley's own theological reflection concerning the "inner life" can best be classed under the third of these options and it is the task of understanding this assertion which defines the scope of this study. Wesley would assume that the concern expressed in the first option would also be addressed in his theology, i.e., that since Christianity is the one and only completely true religion, making clear the nature of Christian experience will likewise make clear the nature of universal truth. But for our purposes, there is no need to give apology on this issue. Let us, therefore, bracket-out the meta-question of Christianity's superiority over the other world religions, along with any concern to compare religious experiences across cultures.

### The Method of This Study

If we take seriously the idea of enunciating Wesley's *vision*, we must first reject the idea of doing a narrow study in the history of ideas. Our primary purpose will not be to try to "shrink" Wesley's "head" - to try to trace out his intellectual pedigree. His general theological viewpoint *did* have certain parallels with Calvinism (shown by Cell), with Lutheranism (shown by Hildebrandt) and with the early church fathers and the Anglican divines (shown by Outler)[14]. Also, some "Wesleyan" conceptions, such as the notion of a "religious sense," show certain continuities with the thought-forms of Malebranche and Norris (shown by Shimizu), not to mention John Locke and Peter Browne (see Matthews), or the "moral sense" philosophy of Hutcheson (see Dreyer). But demonstrating these historical connections in detail is not part of the present inquiry. Wesley's intellectual context will be referred to only where doing so would shed light on what Wesley is trying to express in some particular case. In Ricoeur's language, this is a study in "teleology" and not "archaeology."[15]

Similarly, the history of interpretation of Wesley's views will not be rehearsed here. According to Richard Heitzenrater, there have been over 300 studies of Wesley made in the last two centuries.[16] An exposition of the variety of opinions contained in such a massive body of literature would not only make for tiresome reading, it would not directly serve our purpose.

Yet I do not wish to depict Wesley's views as a timeless set of abstract truths. We cannot extract him from the eighteenth century into a timeless netherland. Wesley's vision of Christianity *did* have a context, a course of development, a history, and I will attempt to convey the relevant aspects of that history. But I will not attempt to draw a map of Wesley's unconscious or pretend that I know each turn in his spiritual and intellectual journey. In other words, my method is to honor the face-value of Wesley's words in order to understand what he had to say about Christianity and the religious affections. I think that it is only after this is done that the uniqueness and enduring relevance of his thought can properly be assessed.

One final point concerning method. Wesley's conception of religious affections, and how that conception looks on modern analysis, is the point of this study. Making the affections the object of a study will strike some as being inadequate. Should not, after all, a study of the affections be supplemented with studies of Wesley's views of will, reason, memory, etc.? Should not the topic be broadened into the elucidation of "Wesley's Psychology" or "Wesley on the Mind?" Does not the topic call for greater integration, more supplementation, if it is to be more than a narrow and obscure bit of musty research?

It must be remembered that this study is an attempt to understand Wesley's affection-related theology, *not* to do a "theology of the affections." By examining his view of the affections, we have access to the most important features of Wesley's understanding of Christianity, not just some minute aspect of a speculative psychology. We must not let the all-too-common prejudice against discussing emotion in intellectual and theological contexts distort our true purpose in examining Wesley's views of the affections.

This prejudice is part of the reason why Wesley's views on the affections have not been adequately studied up to this point. People tend to think that the affections can not be of any positive value *as affections*, but are only of interest in their negative capacity to cloud judgment or distort reason. Instead of doing this, we need to take Wesley's affection-language on its own terms and see the religious affections as Wesley saw them.

### The Plan of This Study

When trying to organize a large and diverse body of material, such as Wesley's works, it is easy to come up with more than one acceptable strategy. The approach adopted here will be to look at Wesley's corpus in logical units according to the form or genre of the writing. Any historical development or change within forms (e.g., how his views evolved between his earliest sermons and his latest ones) will be noted in the appropriate places.

We will start the study of Wesley where Wesley himself usually started his own work, with the Bible. Specifically, let us examine Wesley's *Explanatory Notes* on the Old and New

Testaments to see to what extent Wesley understood the religious affections as being central to the overall thrust of Scripture. Because of the importance of the Bible for Wesley, and because of the wealth of material available, this exposition will cover three chapters.

After this, we will see how Wesley articulated his affection-related theology through the medium of his sermons. Next we will examine Wesley's abridgement of Jonathan Edwards' *Treatise on Religious Affections*. We will look at this work in some depth since it is an important, though often overlooked, summary of Wesley's views about the role of affectivity in Christianity.

Examining the corpus of Wesley's writings according to genre will allow us to see how this central theme of the religious affections was spelled-out according to the requirements and limitations of quite different media: the short note on Scripture, the thematic elaboration of the sermon, and the extended treatise of the academic-literary world.

All of this source work will, unavoidably, contain much exposition of the primary texts. This is necessary because, by and large, Wesley's views about emotion have received more caricature than attentive understanding. The stereotypes of Wesley as a mindless fanatic or enthusiast will be directly challenged, not by denying his emphasis on emotion (as some of his "defenders" do), but by showing the true way that emotion functions in Wesley's theological vision. Because of this, we must go back to the original sources and pay close attention to *his* views, and be careful not to read him through his interpreters.

In the final chapter, a synoptic overview of Wesley's position on the religious affections will be given. In considering how his views might still be relevant to the post-modern world, the critical questions posed above will be reconsidered and answered. Hopefully, this will result in a sharpened understanding not only of the role that certain kinds of experience played in Wesley's thought, but also help us to determine the role that the religious affections should play in our own contemporary construal of Christianity.

1. Many who have *not* ignored these issues, like Bernard of Clairvaux, Bonaventure or even Søren Kierkegaard, are often exiled from the (often more prestigious) realm of "theology" proper and relegated to the supposed nether-region of "spirituality." Others, like Augustine and Aquinas, discuss the nature of the heart and the affections, but these analyses are often ignored (especially by Protestants). On the necessary inter-relation between theology and spirituality, see my "Relations Between Theology and Spirituality: Kierkegaard's Model" in *Studies in Formative Spirituality* (Volume IX, No. 2, May 1988). For some of the historical precedents of a related part of Wesley's theology, see Forest T. Benner's Ph.D. dissertation "The Immediate Antecedents of the Wesleyan Doctrine of the Witness of the Spirit" (Temple University, 1966).

2. *The Book of Discipline* (Nashville: The United Methodist Publishing House, 1984) 78. The revised, 1988 *Book of Discipline*, which was approved just before this manuscript went to press, reaffirmed the four elements of the quadrilateral as sources and criteria for theological endeavors while also affirming Scripture as the primary authority among these four resources. Directly pertinent to the thesis of this present book, the new *Discipline* also affirms that the real energy and the distinctive emphasis of the Wesleyan heritage are seen in its focus on "practical divinity" - the experiential realization of the Gospel in the lives of Christians (see paragraph 66 "Our Doctrinal Heritage", p. 44). This "practical divinity" was most often described by Wesley, and is still most helpfully described, in terms of the affections of the heart.

3. The United Methodist "Order of Baptism" (number 828, page 4, in the *Book of Hymns* [Nashville: United Methodist Publishing House, 1964]) calls for the "sinful affections" to die so that the "things of the Spirit may live." For more recent work in this vein, see *From*

*Hope to Joy* by Don E. Saliers (Nashville: Abingdon Press, 1984).

4. "System and Method in Wesley's Theology", a paper presented at the Annual Meeting of the American Academy of Religion, 1982.

5. Such a method does not necessarily entail a forced or distorted reading of the historical material. It represents, instead, an attempt to be honest about the agenda which is brought to the historical work. It is not possible to do completely "interest free" historical work. It is possible, and desirable, though, to strive to be self-conscious about one's own interests and the effect they will have on the task at hand.

6. See Calhoun, Cheshire and Solomon, Robert C. *What is an Emotion?* (New York: Oxford University Press, 1984) for a summary of much relevant research and an extensive bibliography on the topic of emotion.

7. See my "Finding a Place for Emotions in Christian Theology" in *The Christian Century* (April 29, 1987).

8. See Saliers, Don E., *The Soul in Paraphrase: Prayer and the Christian Affections* (New York: Seabury, 1980) Chapter 1.

9. *The Uses of Scripture in Recent Theology* (Philadelphia: Fortress press, 1975) 159, 163.

10. Wesley's abridgement of Jonathan Edwards' *Treatise on Religious Affections*, found in Wesley's *Works* (Pine, ed., 1773) vol. 23, 312.

11. See, for example, Yandell, Keith E., editor, *God, Man and Religion: Readings in the Philosophy of Religion*, Part I, section 3 "Religious Experiences and Doctrines", New York, McGraw Hill, 1973, 62-165.

12. See, for example, van der Leeuw's *Religion in Essence and Manifestation* (religion's object is "power"), or Schleiermacher's *Glaubenslehre* (the feeling of absolute dependence is central to religion) or Otto's *Mysticism East and West* (mysticism has two principal, classic types).

13. See, for example, Roberts, Robert C., *Spirituality and Human Emotion*, (Grand Rapids: Eerdman's, 1982); and Saliers, Don E., *The Soul in Paraphrase: Prayer and the Christian Affections* (New York: Seabury Press, 1980).

14. For complete references, see Bibliography.

15. Ricoeur, Paul, *The Conflict of Interpretations* (Evanston:

Northwestern University Press, 1974) 22-23.

16. *The Elusive Mr. Wesley*, vol. 1 (Nashville: Abingdon Press, 1984) 12.

# CHAPTER TWO

## The Man of One Book and One Desire: Scripture, the Affections and Wesley's *Notes* on the Old Testament

In 1730 I began to be *homo unius libri*, to study (comparatively) no book but the Bible. I then saw, in a stronger light than ever before, that only one thing is needful, even faith that worketh by the love of God and man, all inward and outward holiness; and I groaned to love God with all my heart, and to serve Him with all my strength."

Wesley's *Journal*, May 14, 1765

### The Affections and the Bible

Some people see the Bible only as a source of rational doctrinal formulations. Others, with a less restrictive view, might say that the Scriptures carry the sacred narrative of God's community, that they tell the great and complex story of the dramatic interactions of God and humanity. What is common to many who hold these (and other) views of the Bible is that the Bible is somehow "out there," and "objective" and, hence, to use it to make reference to one's "inner" life, which is private and "subjective," should be ruled out *a priori* as inappropriate. For such people, all talk which links emotion and the Bible belongs to the realm of "spirituality" or personal devotions, but certainly is embarrassingly irrelevant for theology. For Wesley, such a view misunderstands both the nature of Scripture and the nature of the religious affections.

One is tempted to refute such views about the Bible and emotion, and thereby pave the way for Wesley's analysis, by simply opening up a Biblical concordance at any one of a number of words (e.g., "love," "joy," "heart," etc.) to show the large number of times such terms are employed by the authors of Scripture. But instead of justifying Wesley's affectional exegesis in such a manner, let us allow Wesley's exposition to speak for itself. When we see just how he does treat the Bible, we can then judge whether or not his emphasis on the affections is being imposed on Scripture--if he brought a distorting perspective to the material--or if he is only manifesting and emphasizing what is already there. Before expositing what Wesley thought the Bible taught about the affections it might be helpful to grasp Wesley's overall view of Scripture.

### The Importance of Scripture for Wesley

Most Western churches had, by the seventeenth century, a decisive theological mentor to whom appeal could be made for the final answer on any important issue of the faith. The Romans could look to St. Thomas Aquinas, the Lutherans to Luther, the Reformed church to Calvin. But such was not the case for the Church of England.

Of course, this does not mean they were without doctrinal standards. The Thirty-nine Articles together with the *Homilies* and the standard rubrics of the *Book of Common Prayer* formed a solid conceptual structure where the faith could be housed. But such a corpus of material is always in need of interpretation, and not even Richard Hooker's *Laws of Ecclesiastical Polity* were recognized as a decisive authority.

In the absence of any one dominant system of thought, a consensus had formed by the seventeenth century in the Anglican church that the sources for theological judgment were primarily Scripture and ancient tradition.[1] With the dawning of the Enlightenment in the eighteenth century, reason joined Scripture and tradition to form a normative troika, though the relative authority given to any of these was always a source of debate.[2] This, in broad terms, was the theological setting into which Wesley was born.

### The Task of Interpretation

Having strong minded parents who came from Dissenting backgrounds[3], there could be little question that for John Wesley, it would be the Bible that would always hold the place of honor in questions theological, with tradition and reason serving as its handmaids, not its adjudicators. Indeed, in one of his early letters to his mother he stated "I am...at length come over entirely to your opinion, that saving faith (including practice) is an assent to what God has revealed because He has revealed it, and not because the truth of it may be evinced by reason."[4] The style of interpretation to which he was heir is precisely summarized by Hans Frei: "Biblical interpretation became an imperative need, but its direction was that of incorporating extra-biblical thought, experience and reality into the one real world detailed and made accessible by the biblical story--not the reverse."[5]

If, at one point in his youth, Wesley thought he relied too much on reason (as shown above), at another point he felt himself to be too dependent on tradition in interpreting Scripture. In his *Journal* of January 1738 he confessed that he had "bent the bow too far the other way" by, among other things, "making antiquity a co-ordinate rather than subordinate rule with Scripture."[6] He was never to abandon, though, the riches to be found in the early church fathers.[7]

In making clear just how Scripture and tradition were to be related, Wesley stated "In all cases, the Church is to be judged by the Scripture, not the Scripture by the Church. And Scripture is the best expounder of Scripture. The best way, therefore, to understand it, is carefully to compare Scripture with Scripture, and thereby learn the true meaning of it."[8] He explains elsewhere that if any passage is not to be perverted, the context in which it appears must be taken into account,[9] and that the literal sense is to be followed unless such a reading "implies an absurdity."[10] But even such cautions are not always sufficient to yield a good understanding of Scripture, and it is at such a point where Wesley found the church fathers to be most helpful.

In his "Address to the Clergy" of February 6, 1756, Wesley said that the fathers are

> the most authentic commentators on Scripture, as being both nearest the fountain, and eminently endued with that Spirit by whom all Scripture was given. It will be nicely perceived, I speak chiefly of those who wrote before the council of Nice. But who would not likewise desire to have some acquaintance with those that followed them? With St. Chrysostom, Basil, Jerome, Austin; and, above all, the man of a broken heart, Ephraim Syrus?[11]

He reaffirmed this view in a letter late in his life: "I regard no authority but those of the Ante-Nicene Fathers; nor any of them in opposition to Scripture."[12]

### The Nature and Uses of Scripture

Though he sometimes resorted to bibliomancy when all else failed in the decision-making process,[13] Wesley was not, in general, naive about how the Bible could be used. He once said that "scarce ever was any heretical opinion either invented or revived except Scripture was quoted to defend it."[14]  His high regard for Scripture and his many cautions about its correct interpretation are both a reflection of his rather sophisticated view of the nature of Scripture.  For Wesley, the Bible was an inspired, but also a human, document which was always destined to be interpreted by none but quite fallible human beings.

While some scholars have argued that Wesley was a kind of proto-fundamentalist, holding that the Bible was infallible and inerrant,[15] others have shown that his position was more complex.  William J. Abraham, for one, has shown that Wesley can be shown to have had both a dictationist *and* a functionalist understanding of the nature of Scripture.[16] Abraham argues that Wesley kept these two conceptions in a creative tension with one another (though Wesley's followers usually lost the tension by opting for one side or the other).  We can appreciate the subtlety of Wesley's view when we look at some of his published statements concerning the Bible.

In his abridgement of the *Book of Common Prayer* for the American Methodists in 1784, Wesley reduced the Thirty-Nine Articles of the Church of England down to 24, omitting 6 and combining and altering most of the others. Those two that relate directly to Scripture, though, were, in large part, retained.  Wesley condensed articles number 6 and 7 into one (number 5 of the 24) and omitted only the commendation and listing of the Apocryphal books.[17] Basically what he asserted in this edited article is that Scripture contains all things necessary to salvation and that the Old Testament is not contrary to the New, although Christians are excused from obedience to the Hebrew ceremonial law.

Such a statement would seem to indicate a very high view of Scripture, and this was in fact the case in many ways.

But in the same Sunday service book, Wesley made some other emendations which would indicate a more qualified regard for the Bible. In his Preface, he admits that he left out many Psalms (34 to be exact, and parts of 58 others[18]) since these Psalms were "highly improper for the mouths of a Christian Congregation."[19] This rejection of such a large part of the Psalter for devotional purposes shows that Wesley held something other than a wooden, fundamentalist view of the Bible.

While Wesley did refer to the infallibility of the Bible on several occasions,[20] from his own editorial practice it is clear that when he did so, he was referring only to the original Greek texts. This can be seen in his own translation of the New Testament which contains about 12,000 changes from the Authorized version (many of which were later adopted by the R.S.V.).[21] It is clear that Wesley held that the received text was full of many correctable errors.

His complex view of Scripture can also be seen in his comments on specific biblical verses. In his notes on Revelation, for instance, (which he appropriated almost word-for-word from Johannes Bengel[22]) he does not hesitate to assign literal, historical dates to the author's symbolic utterances:

> Twelve hundred and sixty days--So many prophetic days, which are not, as some have supposed, twelve hundred and sixty, but seven-hundred and seventy-seven, common years. This Bengelius has shown at large in his German Introduction. These we may compute from the year 847 to 1524.[23]

Yet later, commenting on the same book, he vitiates such a rigidly literal view with this comment on Revelation 20:2: "How far these expressions are to be taken literally, and how far figuratively only, who can tell?"[24]

In other places in his New Testament *Notes* he betrays a nuanced understanding of the text which would not be foreign to modern interpreters. Commenting on Acts 7:55 ("But he, looking steadfastly up to heaven, saw the glory of God") Wesley says "Doubtless he saw such a glorious representation, God miraculously operating on his imagination, as on Ezekiel's, when he 'sat in his house at Babylon,' and saw Jerusalem, and seemed to himself 'transported thither' (Ezek. viii: 1-4)."[25] Pre-figuring the twentieth century fascination with the nature of Biblical language, Wesley comments on the parables in Matthew by noting that:

> "This way of speaking, extremely common in the eastern countries, drew and fixed the attention of many, and occasioned the truth delivered to sink the deeper into humble and serious hearers. At the same time, by an awful mixture of justice and mercy, it hid them from the proud and careless."[26]

As a summary of Wesley's approach to Scripture, we may take his comment on Revelation 4:2 as representative: "Here commentators divide: some proceed theologically; others, historically; whereas the right way is, to join both together."[27] For Wesley, the Bible was straightforwardly "sufficient to salvation" and yet still complexly intricate. Theology, history, linguistic skills and many other resources could all aid in the discernment of the meaning of the Scriptures, yet the Gospel was always accessible even to the untutored if the Holy Spirit was guiding the understanding. With this picture of his high, though undogmatic, view of Scripture as a backdrop, we can now proceed to look at Wesley's *Notes* on the Bible.

### The *Notes* in Overview

John Wesley first published his *Explanatory Notes Upon the New Testament* in 1756. This work went through several revisions and many different printings from that time up to the present,[28] due in part, no doubt, to the fact that it was recognized as a doctrinal standard for all Methodist preachers.[29] His *Explanatory Notes Upon the Old Testament* met a quite different fate. Richard Green records that after its publication in installments over a period of three years (1765-7), this work was received with little enthusiasm and that at Wesley's death 750 unsold sets remained in the Methodist Book Room.[30] Yet despite their different histories, both works have several things in common and both are rich sources for understanding Wesley's theology.

It is important to observe that both of these books were called "notes" and the use of the word "commentary" was specifically avoided. The reason for this can be seen in the Preface to his New Testament *Notes*:

> I have endeavored to make the notes as short as possible, that the comment may not obscure or swallow up the text; and as plain as possible, in pursuance of my main design, to assist the unlearned reader. For this reason I have studiously avoided, not only all curious and critical inquiries, and all use of the learned languages, but all such methods of reasoning and modes of expression as people in common life are unacquainted with. For the same reason as I rather endeavor to obviate than to propose and answer objections, so I purposely decline going deep into many difficulties, lest I should leave the ordinary reader behind me.[31]

This theme is echoed over 11 years later in his Preface to his Old Testament *Notes*:

It is not my design to write a book, which a man may read separate from the Bible: but barely to assist those who fear God, in hearing and reading the Bible itself, by shewing the natural sense of every part, in as few and plain words as I can....Sure I am, that tracts wrote in the most plain and simple manner, are of infinitely more service to me, than those which are elaborated with the utmost skill, and set off with the greatest pomp of erudition....But it is no part of my design, to save either learned or unlearned men from the trouble of thinking. If so, I might perhaps write Folios too, which usually overlay, rather than help the thought. On the contrary, my intention is, to make them think, and assist them in thinking.[32]

It was Wesley's desire not to come between the Scriptures and the reader, but to put the reader in more intimate connection with scriptural truth. Hence "*Notes*" and not "Commentary" for the titles of his books.

Another element that both *Notes* have in common is that they are both largely abridgements of the works of other authors. In the Preface to his *Notes on the New Testament* (henceforth "N.T. *Notes*"), Wesley acknowledges using the works of four different men in the preparation of his text. The primary influence was apparently "Bengelius" (the German Johannes Bengel), but he also consulted works of three of his own countrymen: Dr. John Heylyn (whom, according to the *Dictionary of National Biography*, was called the "Mystic Doctor"[33]), John Guyse, an independent minister, and the great non-conformist divine Philip Doddridge.[34]

Wesley at first considered footnoting every borrowing but ultimately decided against it. The reason for this decision hearkens back to his original desire to produce a simple aid for the believer: "I resolved to name none, that nothing might divert the mind of the reader from keeping close to the point in view, and receiving what was spoke, only according to its own intrinsic value."[35]

The same procedure was followed with his *Notes* on the Old Testament (henceforth, "O.T. *Notes*"). In his Preface to that work, Wesley states the he has relied upon two Englishmen: the non-conformist Matthew Henry and the Presbyterian Matthew Poole.[36] At first he was only going to produce an abridgement of Henry's work, and his comments on Genesis and Exodus do come mainly from Henry. But then he discovered Poole's work and the remainder of the *Notes* comes mostly from Poole. Robert Casto has done an exhaustively thorough, line-by-line analysis of the O.T. *Notes* and has determined that Wesley's original material was less than one percent (0.83%), Poole's material was about 70% of the book and the remainder was Henry's work.[37]

The fact that Wesley's two main works concerning the Bible were abridgements is clearly worthy of note, but should not be seen as detrimental to our task of discerning Wesley's own views about the religious affections and Scripture. While he took over vast passages of the work of others, his appropriation was a critical one. As we shall see below, Wesley was careful to excise anything which he thought to be theologically objectionable. On the occasions when he retains and reproduces a questionable comment, he usually enters into a debate with the author in the text of the comment itself. The fact that Wesley put his own name to these works is endorsement enough for our purposes.

In any case, the fact that these are abridgements would be relevant only if there were numerous contradictions in the text itself, in which case discerning Wesley's true view might become a matter of textual criticism. Such was not the case when it came to the topic of the religious affections. In both *Notes*, Wesley stated strongly and consistently that the religious affections are a central and indispensable element of Christianity.

Though his O.T. *Notes* were published 11 years after his N.T. *Notes*, I choose to examine them first. This I do for two reasons. First, they are historically less significant, never achieving, in either Wesley's mind or in those of subsequent church leaders, the normative status for the Methodists that the N.T. *Notes* did. Secondly, it makes Biblical sense to deal with Wesley's view of the Old Testament before proceeding to his views of the New. As far as I can determine, this temporal inversion does no violence to the correct portrayal of Wesley's views. His views on the religious affections remained essentially unchanged over this period of time.

### The Religious Affections and the Old Testament

John Wesley had no pretensions about understanding the entire Old Testament. In his preface to the O.T. *Notes* he says that at first he objected to writing the work because "...there were many passages in the Old, which I did not understand myself, and consequently could not explain to others, either to their satisfaction, or my own."[38]  This uncertainty can also be seen in several places in the text as well, such as Genesis 4:22f: "Why Naamah is particularly named, we know not:  probably they did, who lived when Moses wrote. [v.23] This passage is extremely obscure. We know not whom he slew or on what occasion..."[39]  Or, later, in the introduction to Hosea, he states that Hosea "is the most obscure of all [prophets]."[40]

Such hermeneutical problems were not ultimately serious, however, for the real meaning of the Old Testament was to be found by reading it in light of the New Testament. In his abridged *Articles of Religion* Wesley writes "The Old Testament is not contrary to the New;  for both in the Old and New Testament everlasting life is offered to mankind in

Christ, who is the only Mediator between God and Man, being both God and Man."[41] Because the New Testament is conceptually determinative for Wesley, we need not fill much space with an exposition of his theology of the Old Testament. However, Wesley does make several significant statements, beginning with his Preface, about the importance of religious affections in this work which are worthy of note.

After explaining in his Preface that this work is by and large an abridgement, Wesley proceeds to show how this work is to be used as a practical tool for the believing Christian:

> This is the way to understand the things of God; *Meditate thereon day and night*; so shall you attain the best knowledge; even to *know the only true God and Jesus Christ whom He hath sent*. And this knowledge will lead you, *to love Him, because he hath first loved us*: yea, *to love the Lord your God with all your heart, and with all your soul, and with all your mind, and with all your strength*. Will there not then be all *that mind in you, which was also in Christ Jesus*? And in consequence of this, while you joyfully experience all the holy tempers described in this book, you will likewise be outwardly *holy as He that hath called you is holy in all manner of conversation*.[42]

There are several things to be noted here. First of all, the teleological flow of the discourse. Searching the Scriptures, the task in which Wesley is attempting to assist, is undertaken not for its own sake but for two definite purposes: 1) joyfully to experience the holy tempers described in Scripture, and 2) to be outwardly as holy as God. Since (as we will see in the course of the exposition) the words "temper" and "affection" are used interchangeably by Wesley, he is saying here that achieving certain affections and outward holiness are the true ends of Christian devotion and therefore the true end of the Christian life.

While it should be emphasized that the affections and outward holiness *are* conceptually linked for Wesley, it is important at this juncture to see that the affections are not merely an instrument to achieve outward holiness, they are not just a necessary way-station on the road to social engagement. While it is their nature to lead to outward action, they are to be sought for themselves. To put this another way, we can say that for Wesley, correct outward action in the society of others is a necessary component of Christianity, but not the only one. Meditating on the Scriptures should result in *two* necessary things occurring and Wesley here implies no reductionism of one to the other.

Note here also that while one of the goals is the development of certain affections, the course to be followed in attaining the goal is not mystagogic or ecstatic, but is an easily understandable, rational one. To "understand the things of God" one is to meditate on them, which will lead to knowledge, which will lead to love of God, which leads to the mind of Christ, which produces the holy tempers and outward holiness. Here is our first clue that the religious affections are not merely inner, subjective feelings, but instead are complex entities patterned by the reasoning process.

One final word about this passage from Wesley's Preface. Notice that love of God is the first effect of gaining knowledge of the things of God. The holy or religious tempers or affections flow from this primary affection of love of God. We will see again and again in our exposition that the love of God is the affective context in which all the other affections exist. Gratitude, awe and fear, joy, peace and all the rest seem to be somehow latent in this complex phenomenon called love. We will explore this logic or patterning of the Christian's emotional life in more depth below.

Let us now look to the actual text of the O.T. *Notes* for further indications of Wesley's views concerning the religious affections. Because of Robert Michael Casto's careful analysis of Wesley's O.T. *Notes*, it is possible to classify the passages of comment found in this book into three different categories: 1) those passages Wesley took over word for word, or nearly so, from Henry and Poole; 2) those passages wherein he significantly altered his sources; and 3) those passages which are uniquely the work of Wesley himself. Since his work on the Old Testament is less important both theologically and historically than his work on the New Testament, I think we are justified in focusing our attention mainly on the passages which fall into categories 2 and 3. Those passages that he changed or added show very clearly just how important the religious affections were to his conception of Christianity. We will first look at Wesley's conception of the "heart," that metaphor for the spiritual center of the human being, and then move on to see how he values certain specific religious affections.

**The Heart**

Wesley intervened with his own comments in his O.T. *Notes* most frequently when he thought a passage - in either the text itself or the comment of Henry or Poole - could be interpreted in a Calvinist way. Specifically, whenever he saw indications of unconditional election, limited atonement, irresistible grace, or the necessary perseverance of the saints he took up his pen and set out to battle. Of special interest to us is the fact that many of these controverted passages deal specifically with the nature of the heart.

The issue first arises in Exodus where, on several occasions, Pharaoh's heart is "hardened." Commenting on 4:21 (where God says to Moses "I will harden his heart") Wesley states "After he has frequently harden'd it himself, willfully shutting his eyes against the light, I will at last permit Satan to harden it effectually."[43] Later, commenting on 7:13 ("and he hardened Pharaoh's heart") Wesley says "That is, permitted it to be hardened." In 8:15 ("But when Pharaoh saw that there was a respite, he hardened his heart") Wesley points out that "he did it himself, not God, any otherwise than by not hindering." In 8:19 ("But Pharaoh's heart was hardened") Wesley adds "By himself and the devil."[44]

The same theme arises in Deuteronomy 2:30 where the text reads "hardened his spirit" and Wesley adds "That is, suffered it to be hardened." Likewise in Psalms 105:25 ("He turned their heart to hate his people") Wesley says "That is suffered them to be turned." Wesley makes the same kind of qualifying remarks twice in his comment on Ezekiel, once in his comment on Joel and again on Zechariah.[45]

The importance of these passages is twofold. First of all, we need to note that it is on passages concerning the heart, the spirit, the "inner" arena, that Wesley chooses to make his stand against Calvinistic double-predestinarianism. Showing that God is never the source of evil through his comments on language about the heart, Wesley is saying that language concerning the heart can, and does, touch on issues fundamental to the faith.

Secondly, by making the editorial comments that he did, Wesley is saying that even the heart, that most mysterious entity of the human being, is, at least to some extent, in our control. The hearts of the Biblical figures never were hardened or turned, according to Wesley, without at least the complicity of the person himself. Humanity's freedom extends into the very inner life of the heart.

So far, then, we can say two things about the heart on Wesley's view. First, the heart is crucial for Christianity. It is not the source of irrelevant impulses or merely irrational passions which need to be tamed. It is the arena of the individual person where Christian truth is either exhibited or found wanting.

Secondly, the heart is our own construction. Now, of course, nothing is ever totally our own construction for Wesley, and this is why the epithet "Arminian" does not truly fit his theology. God's prevenient grace, according to Wesley, goes before us in everything we do. Charles Rogers' dissertation "The Concept of Prevenient Grace in the Theology of John Wesley"[46] shows this beyond doubt. But in our freedom, we can determine, and therefore are responsible for, the frame, the contents, the intentions, of our heart. The shape or form of our heart rests on our own evaluations, judgments and decisions.

A corollary to this is that we can never totally suspend our judgment and rely only on intuitive impulses from our heart. There is no built-in guarantee that the heart will be right. This position, implied in Wesley's statements, finds the strongest possible support in the Old Testament literature.

Throughout the Old Testament, when the Lord looks in judgment upon a human, it is not the outward appearance that is considered but the heart (I Sam. 16:7, I Chron. 28:9, Psalm 7:9, Jer. 11:20, 17:10, 20:12). This implies that the heart is not beyond the reach of human moral agency in some unfathomable darkness but is in fact the center of moral agency. That a right heart is not some innate quality or some necessarily present "depth dimension" is seen clearly in the prayer of I Kings 3:9: "Give therefore thy servant an understanding heart, to judge thy people, that I may discern between good and bad..."[47]

Both the tendency of the unregenerate heart toward evil, and the possibility for it to change for the good are seen in Jeremiah. In 17:9 we find "The heart is deceitful above all things and desperately wicked: who can know it?" But in 31:33 we read "But this shall be the covenant that I will make with the house of Israel, After those days, saith the Lord, I will put my Law on their inward parts, and write it in their hearts, and will be their God, and they shall be my people." Similar passages can be found throughout the Scriptures, for example Ezekiel 36:26 which reads "A new heart also will I give you, and a new spirit will I put within you: and I will take away the stony heart out of your flesh, and I will give you a heart of flesh."

In Judges 21:25 we can see the insufficiency of the solitary human, the need for correction from outside of ourselves: "In those days there was no king in Israel; every man did that which was right in his own eyes." On this passage, Wesley comments "What wonder was it then, if all the wickedness overflowed the land?" This shows that for Wesley, endless rummaging in our psyches is no guarantee of knowing the truth about God and what He has done for us. Introspection will only help us to know what we have already formed our hearts to be. The heart does not hold all truth, it holds only what we allow into it.[48]

This means that self-deception is always a possibility for Wesley, and this is a theme we will see again and again. It is because the heart is quite fallible (not to mention the fact that we can and do often go against the leadings of our heart) that the act of repentance is so important, both liturgically and personally, for Wesley. This fact of human nature also necessitates the character trait of humility which is a quality we will see Wesley recommend on many occasions.

To summarize Wesley's O.T. *Notes* on the heart, then, we can say the following. The heart is of central importance for Christianity, but to say this is not to exalt some necessarily and universally present set of norms and criteria for behavior. The heart can be many things, some good, some bad, but its ultimate nature and direction are directly affected by the human agent: for evil if guided only by the human, for good if the Holy Spirit is sought as its ruler.

To assert this of Wesley does not mean that he is an irrelevant eighteenth century curiosity who held that the blood-pumping muscle we know as the heart held mystical sway over the human being. Wesley used "heart" in the same metaphorical way that we do, to signify that part of the human which is most central, most important, the seat of values, the home of the deep and abiding emotions. Regarding the use of this term, we are no more primitive or advanced than Wesley. We still need to refer to our metaphorical center with some such term.[49]

With this understanding of the heart as a background, we can now move on to consider what Wesley saw in the Old Testament regarding the specific affections of the heart. For this, we will start by turning to the largest passage of the O.T. *Notes* which Wesley himself wrote, his comment on the Ten Commandments found in Deuteronomy 5. After this, we will look at a few other related passages of the O.T. *Notes*, before we move on to consider his N.T. *Notes*.

### The Specific Affections

Most of Wesley's original comments in the O.T. *Notes* were a line or two, often consisting of just an alternative translation or a clarification of some minor historical point. But on Deuteronomy 5:7-21, Wesley's comment expands to 171 lines. Because there was no comment on the "spiritual sense" of the Ten Commandments in the notes on the twentieth chapter of Exodus, Wesley thought he should pose a few questions based on the Ten Commandments found in Deuteronomy "which the reader may answer between God and his own soul."[50]

Aside from his comments on verse 19 (thou shall not steal) and verse 20 (Neither shalt thou bear false witness against thy neighbor), Wesley's entire commentary here makes direct reference to the emotions of the believer. These references are not rhetorical flourishes attempting to whip his readers into a frenzy of feeling, but, instead, they are simple, lucid and rational questions about the emotional resources which the reader, as a believer, should (but may not) have. In short, the normative language about emotion is where Wesley's theology is contained. Such language was indispensable, in Wesley's mind, if Christianity were to be conveyed. Let us look at some examples.

Considering the first commandment - Thou shalt have no other Gods before me - Wesley says:

> Hast *thou* worshipped God in spirit and in truth? Hast thou proposed to thyself no end besides him? Hath he been the end of all thy actions? Hast thou sought for any other happiness, than the knowledge and love of God? Dost thou experimentally know the only true God, and Jesus Christ whom he hath sent? Dost thou love God? Dost thy love him with all thy heart, with all thy soul, and with all thy strength; so as to love nothing else but in that manner and degree which tends to increase thy love of him? Hast thou found happiness in God? Is he the desire of thine eyes, the joy of thy heart? If not, thou hast other gods before him.

Commenting on verse 8 (Thou shalt not make any graven image) Wesley makes clear that such an emphasis on love, joy, and happiness in no way entails a disembodied "spirit" mysticism, even if God is pure spirit: "Hast thou not formed any gross image of God in thy mind? Hast thou always thought of him as a pure spirit, whom no man hath seen, nor can see? And hast thou worshipped him with thy body, as well as with thy spirit, seeing both of them are God's?"

The affectional focus is again seen clearly in Wesley's exposition of the commandment against taking the name of God in vain. This whole paragraph is a spiral of images whose common purpose seems to be the promotion of awe.

> Hast thou never used the name of God, unless on solemn and weighty occasions? Hast thou then used it with the deepest awe? Hast thou daily honored his word, his ordinances, his ministers? Hast thou considered all things as they stand in relation to him, and seen God in all? Hast thou looked upon heaven as God's throne? Upon earth as God's footstool? On every thing therein as belonging to the great king? On every creature as full of God?

It apparently seemed obvious to Wesley that if God's name were to be honored, it was not moralistic nagging or high-minded philosophizing that was necessary, but simply the presence of a true and humble awe in the emotional repertoire of the believer, formed by targeting the majesty of God.

Regarding the commandment to keep the sabbath day, Wesley asks "Dost thou do no work on this day, which can be done as well on another? Art thou peculiarly careful on this day, to avoid all conversation, which does not tend to the knowledge and love of God?" Here we see the teleology that Wesley first articulated in the Preface: whatever leads to the knowledge and love of God is to be sought, this is what is definitively Christian. The linking of the terms "knowledge" and "love" is also a key point in this passage. Wesley never proclaims a blind love of God, nor does he recommend a disinterested curiosity about the possibility of the existence of some "higher power". For Wesley, if God, the Christian Trinity, is known, then God is loved. If God is not loved, God is not known.

Regarding the honoring of father and mother, Wesley generalizes this out into the wider context of society at large, again with an eye to the heart: "Have ye that are servants done all things as unto Christ?  Not in eye-service, but in singleness of heart?  Have ye who are masters, behaved as parents to your servants, with all gentleness and affection?"  Similarly, concerning "Thou shalt not kill" he goes beyond (without, of course, denying) the usual understanding of murder:

> Have you not *hated* your *neighbor in your heart*?  Have
> you reproved him that committed sin in your sight?  If
> not, you have in God's account hated him, seeing you
> *suffered sin upon him*.  Have you loved all men as your
> own soul?  As Christ loved us?... Have you shewed
> that you loved all men as yourself, by a constant,
> earnest endeavor, to fill all places with holiness and
> happiness, with the knowledge and love of God?

A similar extrapolation is made regarding adultery:  "If thou hast not been guilty of any act of uncleanness, hath thy heart conceived no unclean thought?  Hast thou not looked on a woman so as to lust after her?"

In his notes on the final commandment, Wesley shows not only his emphasis on the affectional life, but also his highly pragmatic streak.  Coveting anything of your neighbor's is not only wrong, it is unnecessary:

> The plain meaning of this is, thou shalt not desire any
> thing that is not thy own, any thing which thou hast not.
> Indeed why shouldest thou?  God hath given thee
> whatever tends to thy one end, holiness....There is
> therefore no room to desire any thing which thou hast
> not.

As if to give one final testimony to the importance of the affections in assimilating the Decalogue, Wesley adds his own comment on the famous summary of the law found in Deuteronomy 6:5. On "And thou shall love the Lord thy God with all thine heart" Wesley says, "And is this only an external commandment? Can any then say, that the Sinai-covenant was merely external?"

All of these comments show that, on Wesley's terms at least, if the Ten Commandments are to be obeyed, one must cultivate certain patterns of emotion. We cannot obey God if certain affectional habits are not developed. Obedience to God and the deepening of the religious affections are mutually generative.

Other hints at Wesley's position on the affections can be found at other places in the text of the O.T. *Notes*, such as Isaiah 55:1 ("Ho, everyone that thirsteth, come ye to the waters...buy wine and milk, without money, and without price"). On "wine and milk" Poole chose only to say that these represent "All gospel-blessings" whereas Wesley further specifies this by adding "in particular, that peace and joy in the Holy Ghost, which are better than wine, and that love of God which nourishes the soul, as milk does the body."

On three occasions, Wesley offers his original comments in order to assert that the presence of a negative, unchristian emotion in the Old Testament literature (such as hate or anger) shows that Judaism is an inferior religion to Christianity. Numbers 12:3 states "Now the man Moses was very meek..." To this Poole questions "How was Moses so meek, when we often read of his anger?" Wesley retains this question and responds "But this only proves, that the law made nothing perfect." He repeats this quote of Hebrews 7:19 in his comment on Jonah 4:9 where Jonah says "I do well to be angry even unto death." Wesley writes "What a speech! Verily the law made nothing perfect!" On Psalm 139:22 ("I hate them with perfect hatred") Wesley writes "See the difference between the Jewish and the Christian spirit!"

We will disagree with Wesley in his desire to exalt Christianity by downgrading Judaism (though in this he was, unfortunately, a creature of his time) but this should not keep us from seeing what is at stake in these quotes. Wesley is here saying that having certain affections is enough to make a person unchristian. Indeed, the common element in the psalms which Wesley edited out of the American prayerbook (see above) is their largely imprecatory character. The presence or absence of certain affections is a test-case of Christianity for Wesley.

There are, of course, many hundreds of references to emotions or affections in the Old Testament which received no particular comment from Wesley. This does not mean that these passages were not important for him, only that Poole and Henry's comments were deemed adequate. It also should be noted that their own comments were rife with talk of the affections. On Deuteronomy 5:6, for instance, right after Wesley's comments about the Sinai-covenant being internal, Wesley reproduces Poole's comments "With all thy heart--With an entire love. He is one; therefore our hearts must be united in his love. And the whole stream of our affections must run toward Him. O that this love of God may be shed abroad in our hearts."

Limiting our remarks to those passages Wesley himself wrote also leaves unexposited those many passages in the O.T. *Notes* where the emotions of gratitude and thanksgiving are portrayed. Some of the classical texts on fear are also thus ignored, as is the fact that more than half of all the Psalms make reference to the human heart. But our exposition has already established several things.

If one is to be a Christian according to John Wesley's standards, the heart must be engaged. Specifically, one must have certain affections and shun certain other affections. Which affections fall into these categories is just beginning to unfold, but we already know that anger and hate are to be left behind while awe and love of God, along with love of neighbor, are emotional requirements for the Christian. These and other themes received much elucidation in Wesley's *Explanatory Notes Upon the New Testament.*

1. See Felix R. Arnott's essay "Anglicanism in the Seventeenth Century" in *Anglicanism*, Paul Elmore More and Frank Leslie Cross, eds. (N.Y.: The Macmillan Company, 1957) lxxii.

2. See Gerald R. Cragg's *Reason and Authority in the Eighteenth Century* (Cambridge: Cambridge Univ. Press, 1964).

3. Ayling, Stanley, *John Wesley* (Nashville: Abingdon Press, 1979) 16-22.

4. Baker, Frank, ed., *The Works of John Wesley* (Oxford: Clarendon Press, 1980) volume 25, *Letters I*, 188.

5. *The Eclipse of Biblical Narrative* (New Haven: Yale University Press, 1974) 3.

6. Curnock, Nehemiah, ed., *The Journal of the Rev. John Wesley, M.A.* (London: Epworth Press, 1938), volume 1, 419. Hereafter, this will be referred to as *Journal.*

7. See Ted Campbell's Ph.D. dissertation, "John Wesley's Conceptions and Uses of Christian Antiquity," S.M.U., 1984.

8. Jackson, Thomas, ed., *The Works of John Wesley* (Grand Rapids: Baker Book House, 1979) volume 10, 142. Cf. "On Corrupting the Word of God" *Works* volume 7, 473, for this Reformation emphasis on the Bible as its own best interpreter. Hereafter, this edition of Wesley's works will be referred to as *Works.*

9. *Works*, 7:470.

10. *Works*, 6:395. Cf. *Works*, 11:429.

11. *Works*, 10:484.

12. Telford, John, ed., *The Letters of the Rev. John Wesley* (London: Epworth Press, 1960) volume 7, 106. Hereafter, this will be referred to as *Letters.* For more on this theme of the Early Fathers in the thought of Wesley, see Campbell's dissertation, cited above.

13. Baker, Frank, *John Wesley and the Church of England* (Nashville: Abingdon Press, 1970) 30.

14. *Works*, 7:470.

15. E.g., McCarthy, Daryl, "Early Wesleyan Views of Scripture," *Wesleyan Theological Journal*, volume 16, number 2, Fall, 1981, 95-105.

16. "The Concept of Inspiration in the Classical Wesleyan Tradition" in *A Celebration of Ministry*, ed. Kenneth Cain Kinghorn (Wilmore: Francis Asbury Publishing Co., 1982).

17. See James F. White, ed., *John Wesley's Sunday Service* (Quarterly Review Reprint Series, 1984) 307-8.

18. *Ibid.*, 33.

19. *Ibid.*, A1.

20. *Journal*, 6:117; Sugden, Edward H., ed., *Wesley's Standard Sermons* (London: Epworth Press, 1955) 249-250 [hereafter, *Sermons*]; *Letters*, 3:345; and 4:369.

21. See Scroggs, Robin, "John Wesley as Biblical Scholar" in *Journal of Bible and Religion*, volume XXVIII, number 4, October, 1969, 415-422; and Cell, George C., *John Wesley's New Testament Compared with the Authorized Version* (Chicago: 1938).

22. See Wesley, John, *Explanatory Notes Upon the New Testament* (London: Epworth Press, 1976) the "Introduction" to Revelation, 932 [hereafter, N.T. *Notes*]; and Bence, Clarence L., "John Wesley's Teleological Hermeneutic," 1981 Ph.D. dissertation, Emory University, 201.

23. N.T. *Notes*, 995.

24. *Ibid.*, 1037.

25. *Ibid.*, 423.

26. *Ibid.*, 67.

27. *Ibid.*, 954.

28. See Green, Richard, *The Works of John and Charles Wesley* (London: C.H. Kelly, 1896) entry number 172.

29. *Works*, 8:331.

30. Green, 132-3. Schmul Publishers of Salem Ohio reprinted this in 1975, and this is the edition to which I refer.

31. N.T. *Notes*, 7.

32. O.T. *Notes*, viii, ix.

33. Stephen, Leslie, ed., *Dictionary of National Biography* (New York: Macmillan, 1896) volume 26, 319.

34. N.T. *Notes*, 7-8.

35. *Ibid.*, 8.

36. O.T. *Notes*, iii-viii.

37. Casto, Robert Michael, "Exegetical Method in John Wesley's *Explanatory Notes Upon the Old Testament*: A Description of his Approach, Use of Sources and Practice," Ph.D. dissertation, Duke University, 1977, 215.

38. O.T. *Notes*, iii.

39. *Ibid.*, 24.

40. *Ibid.*, 2466. Both this and the previous quote were original material inserted into the *Notes* by Wesley.

41. *Sunday Service*, 308.

42. O.T. *Notes*, ix. Emphasis his.

43. I will assume that the Scripture references are enough documentation to find the quotes taken from Wesley's commentaries and, hence, I will not clutter the text with notes referring to page numbers in either the Old or New Testament *Notes*.

44. Cf. note on Exodus 9:33.

45. Ezekiel 3:20 and 18:31, Joel 2:32, Zec. 2:7. For more on his attacks on predestination, see his comments on Joshua 24:16.

46. Ph.D. dissertation, Duke University, 1967.

47. Here and below I will be using the text (KJV) which is found in the O.T. *Notes* for all Scripture references.

48. Today we would want to sound a note of caution on this, aware as we are that the unconscious can exert a strong hold on us. Our history can, and often does, betray our best intentions. But psychotherapy shows us that if we can consciously appropriate our history, it can cease to have a determinative influence on us. Thus, even the most humanistic therapist would ultimately agree with Wesley on this point.

49. Cf. Saliers, Don E., *The Soul in Paraphrase* (New York: Seabury Press, 1980).

50. O.T. *Notes*, 600. The eschewal of objective, universal answers in favor of the more personal and demanding individual challenge reminds one of the edifying writing of Søren Kierkegaard, especially *For Self-Examination* and *Judge for Yourself!*

# CHAPTER THREE

## "St. Paul was No Stoic": Wesley's Affective Vocabulary in his *Notes* on the New Testament

"St. Paul was no Stoic: he had strong passions,
but all devoted to God."

Wesley's comment on Philippians 4:10

The importance that Wesley places on the affections for the correct appropriation of scriptural truth is seen even in the Preface to his *Explanatory Notes Upon the New Testament*. There he states that "An exact knowledge of the truth was accompanied, in the inspired writers, with an exactly regular series of arguments, a precise expression of their meaning, and a genuine vigor of suitable affections."[1] Later in the Preface, he says that the affections conveyed by Scripture, though often ignored, are one of the most important features of the Bible. Speaking about the language of Scripture he states:

> And the language of His messengers, also, is exact in the highest degree: for the words which were given them accurately answered the impression made upon their minds; and hence, Luther says, 'Divinity is nothing but a grammar of the language of the Holy Ghost.' To understand this thoroughly, we should observe the emphasis which lies on every word--the holy affections expressed thereby, and the tempers

shown by every writer. But how little are these, the latter especially, regarded! though they are wonderfully diffused through the whole New Testament, and are in truth a continued commendation of him who acts or speaks or writes.[2]

### The *Explanatory Notes Upon the New Testament*

Because the N.T. *Notes* were designated by Wesley to be (and are still) part of the theological standard of the Methodist movement, they deserve careful, in-depth analysis. I will not, therefore, as in the previous chapter, pay close attention to the question of which material was appropriated by Wesley from other authors and which was his original work. The entire work merits close analysis because of its semi-canonical status, even though I have been fortunate enough to have access to the typescript of John Lawson's forthcoming edition of the N.T. *Notes*, which contains a painstaking analysis of the text similar to Casto's work on the O.T. *Notes*.[3]

This Lawson text shows us, for example, that the extended quote on the previous page was abridged by Wesley directly from Bengel's Introduction.[4] The Baker/Lawson text is, thus, a work of scholarship worthy of note. But to use this work to ignore vast quantities of the text that Wesley edited - by focusing only on those passages which were original to Wesley - would do a disservice to Wesley's recommendation of the entire book. Indeed, even if *all* of the passages which referred to the "affections" (and cognate terms) were shown to come from other authors, this would only prove that Wesley's emphasis on the affections was not idiosyncratic and was held by several other influential thinkers of his day. There is little reason, then, to try to push behind the received text.

The form of a note on Scripture is necessarily a short one, usually just one or two sentences. This fact necessitates my analysis focusing on particular words which Wesley used in the course of his comment, noting, for instance, the different occasions he chose to use words like "affections" or "passions," etc. Such an approach has its dangers, as shown by James Barr in his critique of Kittel's *Theological Dictionary of the New Testament*.[5] One of the biggest dangers is in ignoring the range of uses and the shadings of meaning which the wider context, and the narrative flow, provide as a background to the individual occurrences of any one term.

Awareness of the potential for distortion by forcing a commensurability of all uses has guarded my work throughout. An analysis focusing on particular words need not be distortive if carefully done, and can, in fact, be very helpful for the task of understanding a concept, as long as the distinction between "word" and "concept" is honored.[6] My inductive approach allows for the gradual unfolding of the concept "religious affection" and avoids the problems Barr addressed.

One methodological step I did *not* take is to go back to the original Greek to see if Wesley's affectional interpretation would have been warranted in the original language. Such an approach was eschewed largely because it would have been a book-length study in itself. But it is also true that such a study would not contribute appreciably to our present task. We are only interested in how Wesley used the received Biblical text as an occasion for making comments about the religious affections.

In many places, the affection language Wesley employed in the comment was not necessarily demanded by the content or the intention of the verse under analysis (as seen, for example, in his "spiritual" commentary on the Ten Commandments exposited in the previous chapter). We are seeking to uncover in this study, however, not the original intentions of the authors of Scripture, but Wesley's views about affections. To say that Wesley used a certain text as an occasion to preach about the affections is not to say that he distorted the text. In my view, Wesley did not distort or twist the basic thrust of the Bible in his *Notes*, but this question need not be decided here. For now, we need only remember that it is the comment and not the Bible text that we are examining.

I do not claim that my analysis of affection words in Wesley's comments is exhaustive, as if I had compiled a complete concordance. I do, however, think I have isolated the majority of references which have implications for my study. At the very least, the references I have gathered will have to be acknowledged as representative of Wesley's views of the religious affections as expressed in his N.T. *Notes*.

In this chapter, I will examine several key words and category-terms, in order to show the over-all importance of affectivity for Wesley. There is some overlap and duplication of meaning among these various terms, but seeing their variety, and seeing which he emphasizes and which he does not, will help us to get a sense for the range of emotive terms in Wesley's vocabulary and what is at stake in his use of them.

After this, in the following chapter, we will go on to see what common features we can ascribe to the affections as Wesley describes them. There we will begin to see the nature, function and implications of the affections as Wesley conceives them. Next, we will look at the particular affections that Wesley mentions most in his N.T. *Notes*. This will show how the emotions are related to each other and how the Scriptures give them pattern and form. The affections that Wesley recommends, as well as those he disavows, will both be examined.

Finally, to complete the analysis of the N.T. *Notes*, we will see how Wesley used affection language in this book to express many of his most important theological concepts and doctrines. This will show that Wesley's theology translated into a non-affective mode (i.e., without reference to the affections) ceases truly to be Wesley's theology. The affections were indispensable to his thought.

## The "Affections" and Related Terms

In the course of commenting on Scripture, Wesley had many occasions to speak about all of our inner life in a large, sweeping way. Other passages required detailed attention to one aspect of affectivity, some particular emotion. In this chapter we will focus on those more general, broad passages. Here, as in the O.T. *Notes*, the most obvious place to start is his language about the heart.

## The "Heart"

That the heart is the locus for God's action in the human is found throughout the N.T. *Notes*. On Romans 8:27 Wesley comments that it is the heart "Wherein the Spirit dwells and intercedes."[7] On Colossians 3:2-3 ("Set your affections on the things above, not the things on the earth. For ye are dead and your life is hid with Christ in God") he comments "For ye are dead--To the things on earth. And your real, spiritual life is hid from the world, and laid up in God, with Christ--Who hath merited, promised, prepared it for us, and gives us the earnest and foretaste of it in our hearts."

Echoing an Old Testament theme, Wesley says on Ephesians 5:19 "Singing with your hearts--As well as your voice. To the Lord--Jesus, who searcheth the heart." Similar to this is his comment on 2 Corinthians 3:3: "Written not in tables of stone--Like the ten commandments. But in the tender, living tables of their hearts--God having taken away the hearts of stone, and given them hearts of flesh." On verse 6 of this same chapter he says "But of the Spirit--Of the gospel dispensation, which is written on the tables of our hearts by the Spirit."

Luke 1:13 evoked this comment: "Thy prayer is heard--Let us observe with pleasure that the prayers of pious worshipers come up with acceptance before God; to whom no costly perfume is so sweet as the fragrancy of an upright heart." Similarly, on Acts 15:9 he says "Purifying...Their hearts--The heart is the proper seat of purity." Again, on Luke 3:8 "Say not within yourselves, We have Abraham to our father--That is, trust not in your being members of the visible church, or in any external privileges whatsoever; for God now requires a change of heart; and that without delay."

As in the O.T. *Notes*, though, there is no romanticism about the heart having necessary and unmediated access to the truths of the universe. The heart is not stable and indelible but can change over time: "I have found David, a man after my own heart--This expression is to be taken in a limited sense. David was such at that time, but not at all times...We must beware of this, unless we would recommend adultery and murder as things after God's own heart." (Acts 13:22) And yet, without the heart, there is no true Christianity: "Their heart is far from me--And, without this, all outward worship is mere mockery of God." Again, in Mark 12:33:

> To love him with all the heart--To love and serve Him with all the united powers of the soul in their utmost vigor. And to love his neighbor as himself--To maintain the same equitable and charitable temper and behaviour toward all men, as we in like circumstances, would wish for from them toward ourselves, is a more necessary and important duty than the offering the most costly and noble sacrifices.

The connection implied so far, namely, that between the heart and the affections, can be found in many places. Two specific examples should suffice. Col. 2:13 in the *Notes* reads "the uncircumcision of your flesh--A beautiful expression for original sin, the inbred corruption of your nature, your uncircumcised heart and affections." In his introductory comments to the book of Revelation, Wesley says "It is scarce possible for any that either love or fear God not to feel their hearts extremely affected in seriously reading either the beginning or the latter part of Revelation."

This linking of the heart and the affections leads to the larger question of the logical connections that are implied by Wesley between the heart and the other faculties/capacities/functions of the "inner" life. First of all, there apparently was, for Wesley, a connection between the heart and the senses: "Through the hardness of their hearts--Callous and senseless. And where there is no sense, there can be no life." (Eph. 4:18) On Mark 6:52 he says "Their heart was hardened--And yet they were not reprobates. It means only, they were slow and dull of apprehension."

The heart is also closely linked with the understanding or the mind for Wesley. On Eph. 4:23 he says "The spirit of your mind--The very ground of your heart." The connection is even clearer in his comments on Luke 24:45 which reads "But still they understood them [the Scriptures] not till He took off the veil from their hearts by the illumination of His Spirit." Again on Luke 24:25 "And slow of heart--Unready to believe what the prophets have so largely spoken," and Rev. 2:23 "Shall know that I search the reins--The desires. And hearts--Thoughts."

And yet this intimate connection does not imply a total identification as seen in his note on Matt. 6:31: "Every verse speaks at once to the understanding and to the heart." Even more explicit is his note on Romans 10:10 "For with the heart--Not the understanding only. Man believeth to righteousness..." Against an overly rational reduction of heart language into mind language, we need to see that in some cases, the heart has to be right before the mind can function correctly:

> Unsanctified learning made his bonds strong, and furnished him with numerous arguments against the gospel. Yet when the grace of God had changed his heart, and turned his accomplishments into another channel, he was the fitter instrument to serve God's wise and merciful purposes, in the defence and propagation of Christianity. (note on Acts 22:3)

The conscience is something else that is linked with the heart for Wesley, though "conscience" is a less important term for him in the N.T. *Notes*. Francis Glasson points out that Wesley dropped the only reference to conscience in the Gospels when he deleted it from John 8:9.[8] Though Wesley used the term occasionally in his *Notes* (e.g. Luke 20:20 "Just men--Men of a tender conscience") he did not hold the natural human conscience in high regard, and in fact saw it as a highly fallible, humanly-formed faculty of judgment, which usually acts only to conform us to society. His note to 2 Cor. 1:12 reads "The testimony of our conscience-- Whatever others think of us."

The unreliability of the conscience can be seen in both Matthew's and Mark's depiction of Herod's role in the death of John the Baptist. On Matthew 14:9 Wesley says "And the King was sorry--Knowing that John was a good man. Yet for oath's sake--So he murdered an innocent man from mere tenderness of conscience!" Likewise, on Mark 6:26 "Yet for his oath's sake, and for the sake of his guests-- Herod's honor was like the conscience of the chief priests. (Matt. 23.6) To shed innocent blood wounded neither one nor the other."

The most complete statement about the heart and the conscience is found in his comment on 1 John 3:19:

> And assure our hearts before him--Shall enjoy the assurance of his favour, and the 'testimony of a good conscience toward God.' The heart, in St. John's language, is the conscience. The conscience is not found in his writings.
> [verse] 20. For if *we have not this testimony, if in anything* our heart, *our own conscience,* condemn us, *much more does* God, *who* is greater than our heart [Wesley's interpolations in the Scripture text italicized]--An infinitely holier and a more impartial Judge. And knoweth all things--So that there is no hope of hiding it from Him.
> [verse] 21. If our heart condemn us not--If our conscience, duly enlightened by the word and Spirit of God, and comparing all our thoughts, words, and works with that word, pronounce that they agree therewith. Then have we confidence toward God--Not only our consciousness of His favour continues and increases, but we have a full persuasion, that 'whatsoever we ask we shall receive of him'.

There are two things worthy of note in this passage, the first relating to Wesley's subtle understanding of the Biblical text. Wesley was sensitive to the variety among the many books of Scripture when he noted that the author of this epistle did not use the word "conscience" but in fact used "heart" to express the reality that Wesley referred to by the term "conscience." Wesley saw the flexibility of these terms and yet was able to convey a consistent meaning with them.

The second point to be drawn from this passage is that the conscience can be trusted only if it is enlightened by the Word and Spirit of God. Again, we find no infallible "depth dimension" universally present in natural humanity which can be consulted for ultimate truth. The person who is shut in on him- or herself has no ally in his spiritual quest in the conscience.

Like "understanding" and "conscience," Wesley often links "spirit" and "soul" with the heart. For instance, in Romans 2:29 he states "And the acceptable circumcision is that of the heart--Referring to Deut. 30:6; the putting away all inward impurity. This is seated in the spirit, the inmost soul, renewed by the Spirit of God." His most explicit attempt to make clear the closely linked, though separate, meaning of these terms comes in his comment on Luke 10:27:

> Thou shalt love the Lord thy God--That is, thou shalt unite all the faculties of the soul to render Him the most intelligent and sincere, the most affectionate and resolute, service. We may safely rest in this general sense of these important words, if we are not able to fix the particular meaning of every single word. If we desire to do this, perhaps the *heart, which is a general expression, may be explained by the three following. With all thy soul, with the warmest affection; with all thy strength*, the most vigorous efforts of thy will; and with all thy *mind, or understanding; in the most wise and reasonable manner thou canst, thy understanding guiding thy will and affections.*

### The "Affections" and the "Tempers"

The most common meaning of "the affections" in the N.T. *Notes* is the general orientation of the person. "Lay not up for yourselves--...guard us against making anything on earth our treasure, when we set our affections upon it." (Matt. 6:19) The affections are something quintessentially human, they define who we are. When Acts 21:13 speaks about "breaking my heart" Wesley comments "For the apostles themselves were not void of human affections." Indeed, if a person is judged to be inhuman it is because of the affections that he holds: "Well is he styled a beast, from his carnal and vile affections; a wild beast, from his savage and cruel spirit!" (Rev. 19:20)

Affections as the general orientation of the human can also be seen in the second chapter of Philippians. Here "bowels of mercies" means, for Wesley, "any tender affection towards each other." (verse 1)  Similarly, in the same chapter, "being of one soul" for Wesley means "animated with the same affections and tempers, as ye have all drunk into one spirit." (verse 2)

Wesley, on occasion, also used the word "affection" in the way it is most often used today, to mean warm regard. For instance, Ephesians 5:25 reads "Even as Christ loved the church--Here is the true model of conjugal affection.  With this kind of affection, with this degree of it, and to this end, should husbands love their wives."  But such usages are by far in the minority and the reader must constantly strive to overcome the tenancy to place contemporary meanings on words that Wesley used.

A related instance of this is the term "conversation." On Philippians 3:20 Wesley writes "Our conversation--The Greek word is of a very extensive meaning:  our citizenship, our thoughts, our affections..." He can also load apparently innocuous words with tremendous affective meaning, as he does with "watch" in 2 Tim. 4:5:  "Watch--An earnest, constant, persevering exercise. The Scripture watching, or waiting, implies steadfast faith, patient hope, labouring love, unceasing prayer; yea, the mighty exertion of all the affections of the soul that a man is capable of."[9]  Though occasionally he will use an affection word that is familiar to us (e.g. "emotion" in Rev. 1:7), we have to be sensitive to the peculiar eighteenth century meanings of such terms as "frame" (as in "frame of the soul" - cf. our modern phrase "frame of mind") as well as a peculiar favorite of Wesley's the "tempers."

That the word "temper" covers the same linguistic ground that "affection" does can be seen in the following series of quotes: "Lord I believe--What an excellent spirit was this man of! Of so deep and strong an understanding...and yet of so teachable a temper..." (John 9:38) "But he that soweth to the Spirit--That follows His guidance in all his tempers and conversation." (Gal. 6:8) "They partook of their food with gladness and singleness of heart--They carried the same happy and holy temper through all their common actions..." (Acts 2:46) "The good man--One who is eminently holy; full of love, of compassion, kindness, mildness, of every heavenly and amiable temper." (Rom. 5:7)

The connotation of a general orientation or approach to life can be seen in these quotes, as well as several passages where "temper" is connected with all of the words that "affection" is usually associated with. "Let us walk by the Spirit--Let us follow His guidance, in all our tempers, thoughts, words and actions." (Gal. 5:25) "But Christ liveth in me--Is a fountain of life in my inmost soul, from which all my tempers, words, and actions flow." (Gal. 2:20) "For all have sinned--In Adam, and in their own persons; by a sinful nature, sinful tempers, and sinful actions." (Rom. 3:23) "Thus is the church on earth instructed, animated, and encouraged by the sentiments, temper, and devotion of the Church in heaven." (Rev. 14:1)[10] In all of these, the essential inter-changeability of "affection" and "temper" can be clearly seen.

## "Passion"

One term which has many affinities with "affection" and "temper" as orientations of the person (or states of the heart) is "passion." In some cases "passion" is used as a cognate for affections, for example in Acts 4:32 "Were of one heart, and of one soul--Their love, their hopes, their passions joined." A similar use is seen in the comment on Phil. 4:10 and used as the motto for this chapter ("St. Paul was no stoic: He had strong passions, but all devoted to God"). This can also be seen in Matt. 26:58: "But Peter followed him afar off--Variously agitated by conflicting passions: love constrained him to follow his Master; fear made him follow afar off." But note in this last passage the unsettled, undecided affective context in which "passion" is used. This is a clue to the more usual way that Wesley used this word, namely, as a pejorative description of some affective state.

We can see this in Col. 3:5 "Inordinate affection--Every passion which does not flow from and lead to the love of God," as well as Luke 6:39 "He spoke a parable--Our Lord sometimes used parables, when He knew plain and open declarations would too much inflame the passions of His hearers." Where Paul is speaking about serving the law of sin with his flesh Wesley comments "But my corrupt passions and appetites still rebel." (Rom. 7:25) Similarly Titus 1:7 states that a Bishop must not be passionate and Wesley comments "But mild, yielding, tender." Most explicit on this theme is 1 Thess. 4:5 where Wesley comments "Not in passionate desire--Which had no place in man when in a state of innocence." In using "passion" primarily in negative contexts, Wesley is in line with the early church fathers whom he so respected.[11]

In the context of differentiating affections from passions, Wesley makes one of his most important statements about the nature of the affections which are truly Christian. Commenting on John 11:33, where Jesus sees Mary weeping and then "groaned deeply and troubled himself," Wesley comments "He troubled himself--An expression amazingly elegant, and full of the highest propriety. For the affections of Jesus were not properly passions, but voluntary emotions, which were wholly in His own power. And this tender trouble, which He now voluntarily sustained, was full of the highest order and reason."[12]

Here we see that Christ's affections (and, hence, by the principle of *imitatio Christi* the model for our own Christian affections) are not the random sensations which can come and go without our control but are voluntary, ordered and reasonable. Wesley does not use the mystical language of being lost or submerged in experience of God. The Christian affections have a pattern, a direction, a grammar to them. We will return to expand on this theme below.

Wesley's N.T. *Notes* was full of language about the heart, the affections and tempers and, to a lesser extent, the passions. There are also several other emotion-related words that Wesley used which merit our attention. We need to see these terms in light of the first order language of the affections in order fully to comprehend the role which they play in Wesley's thought. These concepts are "experience," "spiritual sense," "pleasure" or "comfort," and "feeling" or "impression."

**"Experience"**

Wesley has often been called an "experiential" theologian. Especially since the normative thrust of Methodism has been formally summarized as a "quadrilateral" of Scripture, reason, tradition and experience, much has been made of this distinctively Methodist element of "experience." While Wesley may be considered, in one way or another, an experiential thinker, the term "experience," or its eighteenth century cognate "experimental," do not often appear in his comments on Scripture.

Three of the few examples of this usage to be found in the N.T. *Notes* are found in Ephesians and 1 Corinthians.

Ephesians 1:18 reads "That ye may know the hope of His calling--That ye may experimentally and delightfully know what are the blessings which God has called you to hope for by His word and His Spirit." Ephesians 4:13 conveys a similar thought: "Till we all--And every one of us. Come to the unity of the faith, and knowledge of the Son of God--To both an exact agreement in the Christian doctrine, and an experimental knowledge of Christ as the Son of God." On 1 Cor. 1:24 Wesley notes that while others may see Christ crucified as a stumbling block or foolishness, those that are called will "experience, first, that He is the power, then, that He is the wisdom, of God."

The limitations of "experience" as a theological term are clear in these passages. The major drawback, and it would be a decisive one for a practical thinker like Wesley, is that the term is too general, it is empty of actual content. To hear that we might "experimentally know the blessings that we hope for," to have "an experimental knowledge of Christ," to experience that "Christ is the power and wisdom of God" leaves one feeling rather at loose ends. The questions "How?," and "In what way?" come immediately to mind after hearing these injunctions.

The more concrete language of the particular affections bypasses these questions. Love, joy, fear, etc., are direct and specific and can be sought after by directing one's attention to those aspects of reality which evoke them, specifically, in the Christian context, the story of what God has done for us in Christ. While Wesley used "experience" and "experimental" in rather general and generous ways, the best way to comprehend his appeals to "experience" is by tracing-out his discussions concerning specific affections and the logical relations between these affections and their contexts.

"Experience" was part of the eighteenth century thinker's vocabulary primarily because of people like Locke who held that experience is the source of all knowledge.

Wesley agreed with this.  But the "cash value" (to use William James' term) of "experience" in the Christian arena would, for Wesley, typically be some particular affection.


## The "Spiritual Sense"

The term "spiritual sense," like "experience," appears in certain of Wesley's writings and might be taken to be an important element of his "experimental" approach to theology.  The way it functions in the *Notes*, however, is as a hypothesized faculty or organ whose existence can only be inferred from the actual presence of the religious affections. As in most things, Wesley worked from the most real, obvious and concrete to the more abstract - if indeed it served some purpose to talk about abstractions at all![13]  Let us consider some examples from the *Notes*.

Matthew 13:14 reads "Hearing ye will hear, but in no wise understand--That is, ye will surely hear; all possible means will be given you; yet they will profit you nothing, because your heart is sensual, stupid, and insensible; your spiritual senses are shut up; yea, you have closed your eyes against the light..." Along the same lines is Philippians 1:9-10:

> In knowledge and in all spiritual sense--Which is the ground of all spiritual knowledge.  We must be inwardly sensible of divine peace, joy, love; otherwise we cannot know what they are.
> [verse] 10.  That ye may try--By that spiritual sense. The things that are excellent--Not only good, but the very best; the superior excellence of which is hardly discerned, but by the adult Christian.

Similar is 1 John 1:5 "That God is light--The light of wisdom, love, holiness, glory.  What light is to the natural eye, that God is to the spiritual eye." The final example of this kind of discourse comes from Jude 1:10: "But these-- Without all shame. Rail at the things [of God] which they know not--Neither can know, having no spiritual senses. And the natural things, which they know--By their natural senses, they abuse into occasions of sin."

These passages show the "spiritual sense" to be no mystical illative capacity or an arcane window into the mists of eternity granted only to the masters of the inner life, but something present in every simple believer. While the first and last quotes do speak of the spiritual senses in a substantialist, if somewhat vague, way, the middle two quotes give a more explicit picture of what Wesley is trying to convey. Here it turns out that the spiritual sense is inextricably related to such everyday Christian emotions as peace, joy, and love. What this means is that to be filled with love of God, for example, is to have an awareness, a correct knowledge, of that spiritual reality known as "God." To be "inwardly sensible" of this love is to have a spiritual sense. This "sense" is nothing but a construct which is assumed to lie behind the affection. Wesley did not need to make many references to this sense because it is the first order realities (the affections) which he is trying to propagate among his readers, not a speculative, theoretical understanding of the believer's psychic make-up.

### "Pleasure" and "Comfort"

Some thinkers of the nineteenth century, especially poets and others of the Romantic period, thought of Christianity mainly in terms of its ability to produce certain interior consolations, pleasures or comfort. This was not the case for Wesley. Pleasure and comfort played only a limited, contextual role in his N.T. *Notes*. These immediate positive sensations did not provide the basis for any large scale decisions about the theological adequacy of a thought, doctrine or action. They were in no way the end of Christianity for John Wesley. But neither was avoiding them the duty of the Christian, as if being a Christian were the same thing as being a Stoic. Let us consider a few representative selections.

"Redeeming the time" in Eph. 5:16 for Wesley means "...buying every possible moment out of the hands of sin and Satan; out of the hands of sloth, ease, pleasure, worldly business..." If this were to stand alone Wesley could be accused of being a rather severe sobersides, but later in the same chapter he says "But be ye filled with the Spirit--In all His graces, who gives a more noble pleasure than wine can do." In the same vein, Wesley interprets the 20th verse of Philemon ("Refresh my bowels in Christ") to mean "Give me the most exquisite and Christian pleasure." His distinctions about pleasure become clearest in 2 Peter 1:6 where he writes "Christian temperance implies the voluntary abstaining from all pleasure *which does not lead to God*" [emphasis mine].

A similar set of distinctions applies to the term "comfort." While 2 Cor. 13:11 ("Be of good comfort") means for Wesley "Be filled with divine consolation," he says, commenting on Luke 15:14 that trying to satisfy oneself on worldly comforts is a "vain, fruitless endeavor!" Comforts, like pleasure, are recommended only on the basis of whether or not they are "worldly" or "divine," whether or not they are base or lead to God. Colossians 4:11 is another example of looking only to God for the comfort that is worth attaining: "Who have been a comfort to me?--What, then, can we expect? That all our fellow workers should be a comfort to us?"

One final quote on this topic deserves reproducing. Here we can see the nature of true comfort and what it does and does not imply. In 2 Cor. 1:3 we find the phrase "The Father of mercies, and God of all comfort" on which Wesley comments "Mercies are the fountain of comfort: comfort is the outward expression of mercy. God shows mercy in the affliction itself. He gives comfort both in and after the affliction. Therefore is He termed, the God of all *comfort*. Blessed be this God!" The comfort of God, then, is not something which rescues us from all affliction, but it comes to us in our affliction. Such is no simple-minded escapist pleasure. It is more like a reminder of the cross, and it echoes James 1 which speaks of joy in the midst of tribulation.

### "Feelings," "Impressions" and "Impulses"

One might expect the most elemental language of experience - feelings, impressions and impulses - to be rampant in the pages of a book authored by someone who is often dismissingly called a "pietist" or "enthusiast." Indeed, there is some textual evidence that Wesley was concerned to recommend that Christians needed to be constantly filled with certain feelings. The starkest passage to this effect is found in his comment on the last verse of 2 Peter:

> But grow in grace--That is, in every Christian temper....Frames (allowing the expression) are no other than heavenly tempers, 'the mind that was in Christ.' Feelings are the divine consolations of the Holy Ghost shed abroad in the heart of him that truly believes. And wherever faith is, and wherever Christ is, there are these blessed frames and feelings. If they are not in us, it is a sure sign that, though the wilderness became a pool, the pool is become a wilderness again.

Here it is boldly asserted that a certain feeling is a necessary evidence for the presence of faith.

Note, however, that there is no claim for *constant* "blessed frames and feelings." Examining the other germane quotes from the N.T. *Notes* shows us that Wesley's position is that being intensely aware or conscious of certain feelings is only an episodic feature of the Christian life, not a perpetual state. Let us consider some examples.

In Acts 17:27, Wesley writes:

> If haply--The way is open; God is ready to be found; but He will lay no force upon man. They might feel after him--This is in the midst between seeking and finding. Feeling, being the lowest and grossest of all our senses, is fitly applied to that low knowledge of God. Though he be not far from every one of us--We need not go far to seek or find Him. He is very near us; in us. It is only perverse reason which thinks He is afar off.

Wesley is using "feeling" here in a slightly different sense than it was used in the previous quote.[14] But it is important, nonetheless, to note that in this passage feeling is regarded as the *lowest* of the senses. From feeling we can get a sense of the presence of God in some way, a way which reason cannot provide, but such low-level intuitions are hardly saving knowledge.

Related to this, there are three places in the text where an inward "impulse" is mentioned: In Matt. 4:1 "By the Spirit--Probably through a strong inward impulse"; Luke 2:27 "By the Spirit--By a particular revelation or impulse from Him"; and Acts 7:23 "It came into his heart--Probably by an impulse from God." In all three cases, I have reproduced the whole passage, there was no further elaboration on these "impulses."

In Acts 16:7, however, Wesley makes a fuller, more telling comment: "...but the Spirit suffered them not--Forbidding them as before. Sometimes a strong impression, for which we are not able to give any account, is not altogether to be despised." Here we see that these impressions or impulses are hardly the key to his epistemology, they are merely "not to be despised." His was not a theology of sheer intuition and instinct.

Further evidence for the guarded and limited role that "feeling" (as conscious sensation) plays for Wesley's theology is found in Acts 18:5 where he says "Paul was pressed in spirit--The more, probably, from what Silas and Timotheus related. Every Christian ought diligently to observe any such pressure in his own spirit, and, if it agree with Scripture, to follow it: if he does not, he will feel great heaviness." Here the immediate experience is not given any autonomy at all, but is to be followed only "if it agree with Scripture."

Related to this is the intense experience of crying. On Acts 20:37 Wesley writes:

> "They all wept--Of old, men, yea, the best and bravest of men, were easily melted into tears; a thousand instances of which might be produced from profane as well as sacred writers. But now, notwithstanding the effeminancy which almost universally prevails, we leave those tears to women and children."

Here is no ringing challenge to go out and weep, only a bit of gentle irony about the current attitudes toward crying. This kind of intensity of feeling is in no way suggested to be a continuous norm for Christians.

Even more telling is Matthew 4:1 where, immediately after being baptized by John, Jesus is tempted by the devil: "After this glorious evidence of His Father's love, He was completely armed for the combat. Thus, after the clearest light and the strongest consolation, let us expect the sharpest temptations." There is no sign here of a continuity of feeling, an unbroken flow of pleasant awareness. The warning in the last line in fact seems to be a direct statement to the effect that we are not to depend on feeling since it is bound to fluctuate.

The strongest and, I think, most definitive, statement on this whole matter comes in Wesley's comment on 1 Thessalonians 2:17. The Scripture verse reads: "But we, brethren, being taken from you for a short time, in presence, not in heart, laboured with great desire the more abundantly to see your face." This seemingly unimportant passage occasioned the following remarks from Wesley:

> In this verse we have a remarkable instance, not so much of the transient affections of holy grief, desire, or joy, as of that abiding tenderness, that loving temper, which is so apparent in all St. Paul's writings towards those he styled his children in the faith. This is the more carefully to be observed, because the passions occasionally exercising themselves, and flowing like a torrent, in the apostle, are observable to every reader; whereas it requires a nicer attention to discern those calm, standing tempers, that fixed posture of his soul, from whence the others only flow out, and which more particularly distinguish his character.

Here Wesley straightforwardly states it is the "calm, standing tempers, that fixed posture of the soul" which is indicative of character, not the exhibition of, or the self-conscious awareness of, any particular felt reality. In light of this, and all of the above quotes, I think we can safely say that the conditional statement found in Wesley's comment on 2 Peter (that if faith is present, then one will have certain feelings) is not to be taken to apply to all believers at all times. If one is to be a Christian, then one will have the kind of temper or character or affectional make-up from which the particular Christian affections will "flow out," but this is quite different than saying that a Christian is to be forever filled with certain intense sensations.

Now that we have become familiar with some of Wesley's affective vocabulary and begun to get a sense for how he uses it, many questions present themselves. Let us now turn to some of these questions.

1. N.T. *Notes*, 9.

2. N.T. *Notes*, 9-10. Wesley here echoes Calvin when, in the *Institutes* (1, 3, 9) Calvin says that, ultimately, the authority of Scripture is based on the witness of the Spirit.

3. I thank Dr. Frank Baker for graciously allowing me to study this manuscript in his home/library/study in Durham, N.C. This is due to be published in Abingdon's Wesley *Works* series at some point in the future. A quantitative analysis of the text, similar to what Casto did with the O.T. *Notes*, has not been done, but it is clear that Wesley wrote much more original material for his New Testament work than for his Old.

4. Page 7 of the typescript text of the Lawson edition of the N.T. *Notes*.

5. *The Semantics of Biblical Language* (Oxford: Oxford University Press, 1961) Chapter 8, 206-262, especially 218 on "illegitimate totality transfer."

6. *Ibid.*, especially 206-218 on the difference between "word" and "concept."

7. In order to avoid cumbersomely numerous footnotes, I will give the scriptural citation to the verse that Wesley is commenting upon within the body of the text. If a double dash is in the quote, the material before the dashes is from the biblical text, that after the dashes is Wesley's comment. All Scripture quotations are from the text of the N.T. *Notes* (Wesley's revised KJV) unless otherwise noted.

8. "Wesley's New Testament Reconsidered," *Epworth Review*, May 1983, 28-34.

9. Cf. Outler's edition of Wesley's *Sermons* volume 1, 384 on the active and dynamic way that Wesley understood the term "wait."

10. See also John 1:14. and Matt. 12:37.

11. See, for example, *The Praktikos* of Evagrius Pontikus.

12. On this passage, John Lawson notes: "Although Wesley seems to borrow from Bengel, Doddridge and Guyse likewise reflect the idea of Christ's 'voluntary' emotions in an attempt to reconcile the impassibility of the divine with the suffering of the human Jesus.

Doddridge here translates kai etaraxen eauton as 'he voluntarily afflicted himself.'" (514a, typescript text of the N.T. *Notes*.)

13. Rex Matthews in his article "'With the Eyes of Faith': Spiritual Experience and the Knowledge of God in the Theology of John Wesley," points-out that "spiritual experience" received through the "spiritual sense" is one of the three meanings of "faith" for Wesley, along with faith as belief and faith as trust. I agree with this, and I also agree with Frederick Dreyer's evaluation that the spiritual sense is an important aspect of Wesley's thought (see his "Faith and Experience in the Thought of John Wesley" in *The American Historical Review* volume 88, number 1, 30). This does not contradict, however, our observation that this "sense" plays only a limited role in Wesley's *Notes*. Matthews in his paper reinforces the textual evidence which we have found in the N.T. *Notes* that Wesley did not spend a lot of time elaborating this theory of the "spiritual sense" (*Wesleyan Theology Today*, Abingdon Press, 1985, 406-415, a volume celebrating the Bicentennial of the Methodist Church). However, we need not necessarily conclude that Wesley derived this "sense" language primarily from the empiricism of Locke and Peter Browne (as Dreyer does). Richard Brantley (see bibliography) seems to make this association as well. Terrence Erdt has shown that Perry Miller and others who made similar claims about Jonathan Edwards and empiricism ignored the large body of puritan divinity which speaks about the "sense" of the heart and which was written many years before Locke was born. See below, Chapter 6. I think the same argument can be made regarding Wesley and empiricism *mutatis mutandis*, though as a question in the history of ideas, this is beyond the scope of my study.

14. For a contemporary discussion of the difficulties surrounding the variety of uses of the term "feeling," see Gilbert Ryle's article titled "Feelings" (in *Aesthetics and Language*, Elton, ed.) where he differentiates 7 different meanings for the term "feel."

# CHAPTER FOUR

## "The Fixed Posture of the Soul": The Holy Spirit, The Christian Character and the Affections in Wesley's *Notes* on the New Testament

"...it requires a nicer attention to discern those calm, standing tempers, that fixed posture of his soul, from whence the others only flow out, and which more particularly distinguish his character."

Wesley's comment on 1 Thessalonians 2:17

Let us now begin to explore some of the larger questions that are raised by Wesley's affective terminology in the N.T. *Notes*. What, for instance, makes a religious affection religious? Is it a super-natural act of the Holy Spirit, or can the believer claim the religious affection as his or her own production?

The answer to this question was hinted at in the last chapter when we saw that having a Christian affection is not a purely passive experience. But does this then mean that the affections are totally self-generated? Is an affection totally an "inner" phenomenon? Is it complete in itself or does it have logical connections outside of itself to the social world?

In answering these questions, we will first look at the religious affections in general to see what makes them specifically religious. To do this, we will take a look at the question of agency, the role that the human plays in the generation of the religious affections.  Next we will consider the role which reason plays in the affections which will lead us to the question of the susceptibility of the affections to delusion and self-deception.

After these general points are established - points which will apply to *all* of the religious affections  - we will move on to consider the particular affections which Wesley recommends, as well as those he disavows, in the N.T. *Notes*. Finally, we will look at the theological concepts and doctrines which Wesley manifests in the N.T. *Notes*, focusing especially on those that take a distinctive shape due to Wesley's emphasis on the affections.

### The Affections, Natural and Otherwise

Wesley often referred to the fact that Christian and non-Christians alike have a pattern of acquired behavior known as "natural affection."  Human beings were seen as having certain "natural" features simply because they were human.  On Matthew's use of "flesh and blood" Wesley comments "That is, thy own reason, or any natural power whatsoever." (Matt. 16:17)

Though humans were created with certain innate potential, they do not always reach it.  When Rom. 1:31 mentions those who are "without natural affection" Wesley comments "The custom of exposing their new-born children to perish by cold, hunger, or wild beasts, which so generally prevailed in the heathen world, particularly among the Greeks and Romans, was an amazing instance of this; as is also that of killing their aged and helpless parents, now common among the American heathens." Those "without natural affection" are also mentioned at 2 Tim. 3:3.

But even when the inborn affective capacity is developed to its utmost, it is clearly something quite different than the Spirit-formed Christian character:

It is greatly observable, our Lord has so little regard for one of the highest instances of natural virtue, namely, the returning love for love, that He does not even account it even to deserve thanks. For even sinners, saith He, do the same; men who do not regard God at all. Therefore he may do this who has not taken one step in Christianity. (Luke 6:32)

This theme is also seen in Eph. 4:22: "The old man--That is, the whole body of sin. All sinful desires are deceitful; promising the happiness which they cannot give"; in 1 Peter 1:14: "Your desires--Which ye had while ye were ignorant of God"; and in Philippians 4:5: "Those of the roughest tempers are good-natured to some, from natural sympathy and various motives; a Christian, to all." It is even possible to love Christ "after the flesh" with a "natural love," but when "All things are become new--He has new life, new sense, new faculties, new affections, new appetites, new ideas and conceptions." (2 Cor. 5:16-17)
The relationships between the natural and the religious affections are complex, though. For instance, it is not always the case that grace simply strengthens the natural affections already in place: "He was afraid--Though he had been used to the sea, and was a skillful swimmer. But so it frequently is. When grace begins to act, the natural courage and strength are withdrawn." (Matt. 14:30) Other affections are transmuted: "Christianity ... neither takes away nor embitters, but sweetly tempers, that most refined of all affections, our desire of or love to the dead." (1 Thess. 4:13)
Wesley also held that there is no need for an ongoing drama of alternation between God-given faith and "natural" human despair as, for example, some existentialist thinkers would have us believe:

Ye now therefore have sorrow--This gives us no manner of authority to assert, all believers must come

> into a state of darkness. They never need lose either
> their peace or love, or the witness that they are the
> children of God. They never can lose these, but either
> through sin, or ignorance, or vehement temptation, or
> bodily disorder. (John 16:22)

It is at least possible, then, to leave some of the negative
"natural" affections behind as the Christian progresses
toward the goal of sanctification.

Let this suffice to show that there is, for Wesley, a
distinct difference between natural and religious affections.
We still need to ask what makes the religious affections
distinctively religious. As a start in this direction, let us
examine the categories of "supernatural" and "the Spirit" to
see if somehow these terms are peculiarly linked to the
religious affections.

### The Supernatural, the Holy Spirit and the Affections

In the course of distinguishing "affections" from
"passions" in the last chapter, we saw that for Wesley the
human is more active, more in control, of an affection than
a passion. Let us now return to this point to see what
implications this has regarding two well-known features of
Wesley's thought, his supernaturalism and his emphasis on
the Holy Spirit. We will begin with the widest possible focus
- the general question about the natural versus the
supernatural in Wesley's thought.

It is clear, first of all, that Wesley was no Deist on this
question. He had a robust appreciation for the phenomena
deemed "supernatural." This most obviously surfaces in his
ironic, and even sarcastic, comments about his
contemporaries who would attempt to read Scripture in a
totally naturalistic way. In Mark 3:22, where the author
speaks about casting out devils, Wesley comments "How
easily may a man of learning elude the strongest proof of a

work of God! How readily can he account for every incident, without ever taking God into the question!" Commenting on Luke 13:11, where a woman was utterly unable to lift herself up, he says "Would not a modern physician have termed it a nervous case?"

In Matt. 10:8, again on the topic of devils, he says "Suppose God should suffer an evil spirit to usurp the same power over a man's body as the man himself has naturally, and suppose him actually to exercise that power, could we conclude the devil had no hand therein, because his body was bent in the very same manner wherein the man himself might have bent it naturally?" Sharper still are his comments on Mark 1:34, "He suffered not the devils to say that they knew him--That is, according to Dr. Mead's hypothesis (that the scriptural demoniacs were only diseased persons), 'He suffered not the diseases to say that they knew Him!' But perhaps the most clear evidence for Wesley's supernaturalism can be seen in his comment on John 8:59 "But Jesus concealed himself--Probably by becoming invisible."

In spite of such statements, Wesley was not always quick to give the most supernatural account of events. On Luke 1:41, for instance, speaking about the baby leaping in Elizabeth's womb, he says "... the joy of her soul so affected her body, that the very child in her womb was moved in an uncommon manner, as if it leaped for joy." Here it is not John who supernaturally recognizes the mother of Jesus, as one might assume from the text, but it is Elizabeth's body which causes the movement.

Similarly, he sees how the natural and the supernatural can go hand in hand in some instances. On Matt. 17:15 he writes "He is a lunatic--This word might with great propriety be used, though the case was mostly preternatural; as the evil spirit would undoubtedly take advantage of the influence which the changes of the moon have on the brain and nerves." We might not agree with his linking of the moon with the behavior of the "lunatic," but we should see that, for his time, this was a naturalistic link which Wesley would not rule out of the explanatory process.

Both his supernaturalism, and the qualified role it plays in his thought, can be seen in his note to 2 Cor. 12:2:

> Whether in the body, or out of the body, I know not--It is equally possible with God to present distant things to the imagination in the body, as if the soul were absent from it, and present with them; or to transport both soul and body for what time He pleases to heaven; or to transport the soul only thither for a season, and in the meantime to preserve the body fit for its re-entrance.  But since the apostle himself did not know whether his soul was in the body, or whether one or both were actually in heaven, it would be a vain curiosity for us to attempt determining it.

This shows that while the supernatural can break into the natural at any time, making the distinction between the two may not always be relevant to the particular case at hand.

If it was not always important to discern extraordinary breaks in the natural causal nexus, it was, nonetheless, crucial for Wesley to be able to name God in a particular situation.  Indeed, the unforgivable "blasphemy against the Spirit" is "neither more nor less than the ascribing those miracles to the power of the devil which Christ wrought by the power of the Holy Ghost." (Matt. 12:31.[1])  That it is possible not to see God where God in fact is can be seen in Wesley's comments on John 6:44:  "No man comes to me, unless my Father draw him--No man can believe in Christ unless God give him power.  He draws us first by good desires, not by compulsion, not by laying the will under any necessity; but by the strong and sweet, yet still resistible, motions of His heavenly grace."  Being resistible, God cannot be overwhelmingly obvious. This implies our responsibility to seek and discern the Spirit.

Such responsibility, the implied necessary activity of the person in the process of discerning God, is seen clearly in John 7:16: "If any man be willing to do his will, he shall know of the doctrine, whether it be of God--This is a universal rule, with regard to all persons and doctrines. He that is thoroughly willing to do it, shall certainly know what the will of God is."

This implies some preparation, some training in the things of God, before one can name God. Seeing certain activity as the activity of the Holy Spirit, then, is a contingent matter, contingent, in many ways, upon our will. Being passive and quiet is no guarantee of engaging, serving, or realizing God. In fact, in some cases just the opposite is true:

> [God] never designed any promise should encourage rational creatures to act in an irrational manner; or to remain inactive when He has given them natural capacities...To expect the accomplishment of any promise, without exerting these, is at best vain and dangerous presumption, if all pretense of relying upon it be not profane hypocrisy. (Acts 27:31)

This position is, of course, well supported by Scripture, for example, Hebrews 5:14: "But strong meat belongeth to them of full age, to them who have sense exercised by habit to discern both good and evil." Spiritual events, then, are not always the result of heaven-rending special revelations, but, we might say, they occur in, with and under the "natural" events and are seen and heard only by those who have the eyes to see them and the ears to hear them. This can also be seen in some of Wesley's remarks about the nature of Biblical language.

On Mark 4:2 we read "A parable signifies, not only a simile or comparison, and sometimes a proverb, but any kind of instructive speech, wherein spiritual things are explained and illustrated by natural."  Similar is the comment on 1 Cor. 1:17: "Lest the cross of Christ should be made of no effect--The whole effect of St. Paul's preaching was owing to the power of God accompanying the plain declaration of that great truth, 'Christ bore our sins upon the cross.'  But the effect might have been imputed to another cause, had he come with that wisdom of speech which they admired."  This shows that, in some cases, the Spirit, far from always manifesting itself in unusual ways, sometimes requires the natural, the quotidian, the unassuming, to accomplish its purposes.

The spiritual or Godly - that which God has a hand in - is therefore distinguishable from the supernatural. Applying this to the affections, we see that religious or Christian affections need not be understood as supernatural and mystical infusions of the Spirit of God.  We can see explicit examples of this by taking a close look at Wesley's language about the "testimony of the Holy Spirit" which shows that the Spirit does not always make a dramatic epiphany, but in fact is often quite subtle.

First of all, we need to see that the inner theatre is hardly the only venue for the "testimony" or "witness" of the Holy Spirit.  "The Holy Ghost witnesseth--By other persons. Such was God's good pleasure, to reveal these things to him not immediately, but by the ministry of others." (Acts 20:23)

Secondly, even when, in the *Notes*, the "testimony of the Holy Ghost" is said to be an "inner" experience, it is usually specified by Wesley beyond its formal, neutral and, frankly, obscure, literal meaning.  Though in 1 Peter 1:12 the "inward testimony of the Holy Ghost" is mentioned without elaboration, it is more common to see this "testimony" translated into other terms, often affection terms.  On 1 John 3:24 he says "hereby we know that He abideth in us, by the Spirit which he hath given us--Which witnesseth with our spirits that we are His children, and brings forth His fruits of peace, love, holiness." On Luke 24:32 he specifies a vague "burning heart" into the more concrete experience of love: "Did not our heart burn within us?--Did not we feel an unusual warmth of love?"

In commenting on Acts 10:38 Wesley notes that Scripture itself has this tendency to further specify the action of the Spirit:

> With the Holy Ghost and with power--It is worthy our remark that frequently when the Holy Ghost is mentioned, there is added a word particularly adapted to the present circumstance. So the deacons were to be 'full of the Holy Ghost and wisdom' (Acts 6:3); Barnabas was 'full of the Holy Ghost and faith' (11:24); the disciples were 'filled with joy and with the Holy Ghost' (13:52); and here, where His mighty works are mentioned, Christ Himself is said to be anointed with the Holy Ghost and power.

This tendency to specify or make more concrete the presence of the Spirit shows us that in those unusual circumstances when we are consciously aware of the Spirit, it is usually as some specific ability or object-related affection and not just an ineffable occurrence in our interior.

In light of all of this, we can say that Wesley's synergistic understanding of the religious affections does not fall neatly into one or the other side of the dichotomies "natural/supernatural," "human/spiritual" or "actively created/passively received." Rather than using each of these terms univocally, Wesley deploys each contrast in specific contexts depending upon what misunderstanding he is addressing. He thus avoids creating a dichotomous metaphysical framework (such as Kant's "noumenal" and "phenomenal" or Locke's "unknowable substratum" and "empirical qualities"). Let us, then, see how Wesley himself spoke about the affections without trying to force his views into some inappropriate shape. To do this, it turns out, involves challenging some of our most strongly held modern preconceptions about affectivity. This is so because, for Wesley, the affections are neither entirely "inner," nor entirely "irrational" realities.

### The "Inner" and the "Outer"

In a few places in the N.T. *Notes*, Wesley interpreted "sincerity" to be a cipher for the whole of the heart's affections: "Sincerity and truth seem to be put here for the whole of true, inward religion." (1 Cor. 5:8) But this usage was relatively infrequent, probably because it sounds as if anything honestly "felt" (held, believed) would qualify as "true religion." Such would hardly be acceptable to Wesley, since Christianity is a specific, contingent pattern of affectivity which also has logical connections outside of the self to God and the world.

There are many cases where Wesley joins together in the same sentence references to both the inner world and the outer world. On Luke 15:31 he speaks about making progress "in inward as well as outward holiness." His note to 2 Cor. 7:1 reads "Let us cleanse ourselves...from all pollution of the flesh--All outward sin. And of the spirit-- All inward." The linkage is seen again in his comment on Rom. 1:25: "And worshipped--Inwardly. And served-- Outwardly."

A slight variation on this theme is seen in those passages where he links the inner and the outer, and emphasizes graphically that the outward aspect of religion alone is not enough. Commenting on Luke 11:44 Wesley mentions that "On another occasion Christ compared them to 'whited sepulchres,' fair without, but foul within (Matt.

23.27)." A similar comment appears on Acts 23:3 "God is about to smite thee, thou whited wall--Fair without; full of dirt and rubbish within."

His view becomes even clearer when we see that not only was outward religion not enough, but that inward religion has a logical priority over the outer. "My kingdom is not of this world--Is not an external, but a spiritual kingdom." (John 18:36)  Again this is seen in Matt. 7:15 "Beware of false prophets...in sheep's clothing--With outside religion, and fair professions of love"; and most clearly in the note to 1 Tim. 2:2 "Godliness--Inward religion; the true worship of God."

But while there were, for Wesley, some legitimate uses of the inner/outer distinction regarding the proper Christian life, the distinction could not be over-arching or systematically universal, for in a very real sense the Christian affections are "outer" as well as inner. This is true in two senses. First, the affections arise from the person being directed, focused, fixed on some object. It is this object, coming to us from outside of our inner awareness, which is in many ways the cause of the affection.[2] Secondly, the affection has its *telos* or proper end, that to which it logically leads or points, outside of the self as well. In other words, having an affection means being disposed to behave in certain ways.[3] Let us now consider these two "outer" elements of the affections, beginning with the fact that they take objects or, in other words, that they are "transitive."

### The Transitivity of Emotion

The N.T. *Notes* are full of references to the fact that emotions take objects and that, specifically, the Christian emotions take God, and what God has done for us, as their object. In Rom. 1:4 we read "By the resurrection from the dead--For this is both the foundation and the object of our faith; and the preaching of the apostles was the consequence of Christ's resurrection." In Luke 11:33 "The meaning is, God gives you this gospel light, that you may repent. Let your eye be singly fixed on Him, aim only at pleasing God; and while you do this, your whole soul will be full of wisdom, holiness, and happiness." On Rom. 1:7 he says "Our trust and prayer fix on God, as He is the Father of Christ; and on Christ, as He presents us to the Father." Later in Romans we see "If we believe on Him who raised up Jesus--God the Father is therefore the proper object of justifying faith." (Rom. 4:24)

That specific affections find their genesis in this way is shown in Wesley's comment on Rom. 1:21: "They did not glorify him as God, neither were thankful--They neither thanked Him for His benefits, nor glorified Him for His divine perfections." Here we see that our thankfulness to God comes from targeting what God has done for us. In the same way, our praise or glorification of God takes God's perfections as its object.

His comment on 2 Cor. 5:13 shows us that even in religious ecstasies, the Christian is not an idiot (in the Greek sense of "idios," "one's own") but is still fixed on God: "For if we are transported beyond ourselves--Or, at least, appear so to others, treated of verses 15-21, speaking or writing with uncommon vehemences. It is to God--He understands (if men do not) the emotion which Himself inspires." Such experiences, if genuine, are not the novel creation of unbalanced people, they are simply the result of realizing who God is and what God has done.

The transitivity of emotion, of course, does not apply only to the religious affections, but also to the natural affections:

> They that are after the flesh...mind the things of the flesh--Have their thoughts and affections fixed on such things as gratify corrupt nature: namely, on things visible and temporal: on things of the earth, on

pleasure (of sense or imagination), praise, or riches. But they who are after the Spirit--Who are under His guidance. Mind the things of the Spirit--Think of, relish, love things invisible, eternal; the things which the Spirit hath revealed, which He works in us, moves us to, and promises to give us. (Rom. 8:5)

Whatever is the object of our attention will determine the form of our heart, the posture of our soul, the nature of our affections. In the words of Matthew 6:21f "For where your treasure is, there will your heart be also. The eye is the lamp of the body: if therefore thine eye be single, thy whole body shall be full of light. But if thine eye be evil, thy whole body shall be full of darkness."

## Society and the Affections

Religious affections, then, are not totally self-contained "inner" realities in that they require an object. Their generation is a result of the soul turning to God. If God is not the object, they are not Christian affections. But this is not the only outward-turning aspect of Christian emotion.

That Wesley himself constantly did good works is well-known to all who have studied his life, and this emphasis on works is also found in the N.T. *Notes*. Commenting on James 2:14, Wesley notes that "James refutes not the doctrine of St. Paul, but the error of those who abused it." He later specifies this by saying "Works do not give life to faith, but faith begets works, and then is perfected by them." (Jas. 2:22) On Acts 27:23 we read "The God whose I am, and whom I serve--How short a compendium of religion! yet how full! comprehending faith, hope, and love!"

The same theme is seen in Matt. 7:16:

By their fruits ye shall know them--A short, plain, easy rule, whereby to know true from false prophets; and one that may be applied by people of the meanest capacity, who are not accustomed to deep reasoning. True prophets convert sinners to God, or at least confirm and strengthen those that are converted. False prophets do not.

This responsibility to be active in the world is also implied in Wesley's comment on John 2:2: "Jesus and his disciples were invited to the marriage--Christ does not take away human society, but sanctifies it."

What may not be as widely recognized as Wesley's emphasis on works is that, on Wesley's terms, these works are to issue from those affections and tempers which come from targeting God with our attention: "He that soweth sparingly shall reap sparingly; he that soweth bountifully shall reap bountifully--A general rule. God will proportion the reward to the work, *and the temper whence it proceeds*." (2 Cor. 9:6, emphasis mine)  In commenting on Matt. 6:1, he says that this chapter is about "the purity of intention without which none of our outward actions are holy." Where James 1:26 reads "Pure religion and undefiled before God even the Father is this, To visit the fatherless and widows in their affliction, and to keep himself unspotted from the world," Wesley comments "But this cannot be done till we have given our hearts to God, and love our neighbor as ourselves."

On this point it should be recalled what Wesley said in his comment on 1 Thess. 2:17, which was quoted at the end of the last chapter. There he wrote about the "calm standing tempers, that fixed posture of the soul" which is the distinguishing sign of the human character. It is the opposite of such dispositions which characterizes the wicked man: "So changeable are the hearts of wicked men! So little are their starts of love to be depended on!" Only the Christian tempers yield the fruits that persevere.

Thus the *telos*, like the genesis, of the affections lies outside of the self. In this sense also, then, the religious affections are not a purely "inner" phenomena. Or, we might say, if they are only inner, then they are not really religious. To love God and one's neighbor, to take joy in the happiness of others, to fear the wrath of God, all imply dispositions to behave in certain ways. We do not seek to serve our neighbor because of some inherent attractiveness of the neighbor, but because of who God is, what God has done for us, and the consequent love and gratitude which are generated in us by these realities.[4] Just as the quality of the object determined whether the affection was truly religious, so the quality of the resulting action is an indicator of the nature of the affection. Though one cannot know the state of the heart *only* by looking at the outward person, the behavior or action ("fruits") of the person is one important indicator of the purity of the heart.

### Reason and its Contrary

Often in popular conception, emotions are considered to be not only "inner," but also "irrational," and, of course, many times they are. But when Wesley spoke about the religious affections, he had no such conception in mind. Again, we must suppress our "common sense" notions about emotion if we are to understand Wesley's position.

Regarding the rationality of Wesley's thought in general, it is true that Wesley had some scornful things to say about natural, unaided human reason. His note on Acts 17:18, for example, reads:

What would this babbler say?--Such is the language of natural reason, full of, and satisfied with, itself. Yet even here St. Paul had some fruit; though nowhere less than at Athens. And no wonder, since this city was a seminary of philosophers, who have ever been the pest of true religion.

Elsewhere he speaks of the "pride" of reason (Acts 17:32) and the instability of reason (Acts 28:6). But this did not mean that he had no use for reason, far from it. The true Christian has reason beyond the ken of the natural man, as seen in 1 Cor. 14:20: "But in understanding be ye grown men--Knowing religion was not designed to destroy any of our natural faculties, but to exalt and improve them, our reason in particular."

This reason that has been "exalted" by religion is very far from being opposed to the religious affections. So far are the religious affections from being "irrational" on Wesley's terms that there is, in fact, a necessary connection between the religious affections and "reason" (or "understanding," "judgment," or the "knowing" faculty - all these terms are used in a roughly equivalent manner in the *Notes*, though they can be differentiated in other circumstances.[5])

This necessary connection can be seen, first of all, in the many passages where the "mind" is said to contain both the understanding and the affections. The note to Col. 1:21 reads "In your mind--Both your understanding and your affections" and that on 1 Peter 1:13 reads "Gird up the loins of your mind--...so gather ye up all your thoughts and affections. "Similarly, the note on James 1:5 refers to the "affections of the mind" and that on 1 Cor. 2:3, commenting on the phrase "in fear and trembling," reads "The emotion of my mind affecting my very body."[6]

That there is "reason," or some engagement of the mind, in the affections for Wesley is seen in his many reminders that knowledge is to direct our tempers or "zeal." On Gal. 4:17-18 he says "Their zeal is not according to knowledge...True zeal is only fervent love." Commenting on Rom. 10:2, he diagnoses the malaise of his age: "They have zeal, but not according to knowledge--They had zeal without knowledge; we have knowledge without zeal." On this same theme in 1 Cor. 14:6 he says "Doctrine--To regulate your tempers and lives."

On Titus 2:4 Wesley speaks about how wives are to love their families "With a tender, temperate, holy, wise affection." This obviously implies the tempering of the affections by the faculty of judgment. This is also found in Matt. 6:9: "Hallowed be thy name--Mayest Thou, O Father, be truly known by all intelligent beings, and with affections suitable to that knowledge!"

The mirror image of this can also be see when Wesley talks about "inordinate affection" in 1 Thess. 4:6, or "immoderate sorrow" in John 16:12. But the role of reason or judgment in the "inner" life of the believer is nowhere clearer than in Wesley's note to 1 Cor. 14:32:

> For the spirits of the prophets are subject to the prophets--But what enthusiast considers this? The impulses of the Holy Spirit, even in men really inspired, so suit themselves to their rational faculties, as not to divest them of the government of themselves, like the heathen priests under their diabolical possessions. Evil spirits threw their prophets into such ungovernable ecstasies, as forced them to speak and act like madmen. But the Spirit of God left His prophets the clear use of their judgment, when, and how long it was fit for them to speak, and never hurried them into any improprieties either as to the manner, or time of their speaking.

Note here also the implied rejection of a solely supernatural or disruptive understanding of the Holy Spirit which we addressed earlier in this chapter.

Wesley is again on solid biblical ground in his emphasis on the constant role of judgment or reason in the Christian life. Passages such as 1 John 4:1 ("try the spirits whether they are of God") and 1 Thess. 5:21 ("prove all things, hold fast that which is good") show that the authors of Scripture never intended Christianity to be an exercise in uncritical intuition.[7] The constant presence of the judging faculty also helps to prevent any easy slide into self-deceptive affective/religious practices.

### Self-Deception and the Affections

There are many examples of self-deception in the New Testament and Wesley is eager to put them to didactic use. On Col. 2:18 he shows that what was thought to be humility was really pride; on Luke 13:16 he points out that the real motive involved was envy and not "pure zeal for the glory of God"; on Luke 16:3 he quotes an uncited source which recognized this tendency to produce deluded evaluations of the self and its motives and affections: "'By men called honour, but by angels pride.'" Even the proceedings of the historical church councils, when they took the form of anathemas, "consecrated some of the most devilish passions under the most sacred names; and, like some ill-adjusted weapons of war, are most likely to hurt the hand from which they are thrown." (Acts 15:29)

Humans being what they are, there can be no once and for all remedies for this tendency, but Wesley does recommend several safeguards. The most general and most important of these comes, not surprisingly, from the pattern set by Christ. In this case, what he is singling out from Christ's life for imitation is the self-denial symbolized in the cross.

Where Matthew states "Let him deny himself, and take up his cross" Wesley comments "A rule that can never be too much observed: let him in all things deny his own will, however pleasing, and do the will of God, however painful." Shortly after this same passage appears in Luke, Wesley writes "In joy remember the cross. So wisely does our Lord balance praise with sufferings."

Aside from this general admonition, Wesley gives several other specific checks against self-deception in the course of his exposition of the New Testament. One most frequently mentioned is Scripture itself. The charge to "try the spirits" is understood by Wesley to mean "We are to try all spirits by the written word: 'To the law and the testimony!' If any man speak not according to these, the spirit which actuates him is not of God." (1 John 4:1) Similarly "prove all things means" "Try every advice by the touchstone of Scripture..."

Other checks to delusion are the reproof of others (Matt. 18:15) the passage of time (Matt. 13:26) and, most importantly, the person's own actions. As shown above, the religious affections imply certain actions in the world, the society of others, and if these dispositions are not present, as shown through good works, then the affections under scrutiny are not in fact Christian. If we shut up our compassion to our brother or sister in need, does God dwell in our hearts? "Certainly not at all, however he may talk (verse 18) of loving God." (1 John 3:17)

Thus the dispositional nature of the affections is the ultimate check against self-deception. This fact, along with the transitive and rational nature of the affections, can all be seen in Wesley's note to Philippians 1:10-11. This will serve nicely as a summary statement of the grammar of the religious affections.

> That ye may be inwardly sincere--Having a single eye to the very best of things, and a pure heart. And outwardly without offense--Holy, unblamable in all things.
> v.11 Being filled with the fruits of righteousness, which are through Jesus Christ, to the glory and praise of God--Here are three properties of that sincerity which

is acceptable to God: (1) It must bear fruits, the fruits of righteousness, all inward and outward holiness, all good tempers, words, and works; and that so abundantly that we may be filled with them. (2) The branch and the fruits must derive both their virtue and their very being from the all-supporting, all-supplying root, Jesus Christ. (3) As all these flow from the grace of Christ, so they must issue in the glory and praise of God.

With this over-all grammar or pattern in mind, let us now look at the specific religious affections which Wesley emphasized, and then go on to see what doctrinal implications these affections had for Wesley's theology.

### The Affections to be Sought and Shunned

The dispositional nature of the affections makes them more like virtues than feelings. In fact, when we see the list (below) of the affections which Wesley mentions most, we will see some terms which might be called "virtues" as easily as they could be called affections. But the main connotation of "virtue" is the disposition to behave, and thus it does not suggest the "transitive" element of "affection," nor the engagement of the heart, the center of experience, that "affection" does. So the only proper term we could assign these terms descriptive of the Christian character is "affections."

This list of affections is not intended to represent a complete and comprehensive guide to the affective life of the Christian. I list here only those affections which Wesley emphasizes. Though the list is not exhaustive, it can be said that if a person embodied all of these, that person would be a participant in the power of God, and Wesley would call that person a Christian.

It would, of course, be impossible to give a complete list of references to places in the N.T. *Notes* where all of these affections are discussed. In the note to each affection I will give only a representative sampling. Some affections, as will be obvious, were mentioned more frequently than others. But even those mentioned rarely were emphasized in such a way by Wesley as to merit their inclusion.

The affection of **thankfulness** or **gratitude** is not often mentioned by Wesley, but it is clearly implied in many of the references to "joy" (see below). Commenting on Rom. 1:8, though, Wesley seems to give it a kind of logical priority: "I thank--In the very entrance of this one epistle are the traces of all spiritual affections; but of thankfulness above all, with the expression of which almost all St. Paul's epistles begin."

Some may think it is odd to think of **faith** as an affection, especially if one is used to thinking of it in the sense of "believe," i.e., affirming certain propositions. Wesley does not deny this sense of "faith" but his conception goes beyond this to the sense of **trust**, trust in what God is, and in what God has done for us (cf. Hebrews 11:1) The most common way it is cited in the *Notes* is in a quote of Galatians 5:6 "faith which worketh by love."[8]

As Wesley notes in Ephesians 6:17, there is a range or spectrum of **hope** to which the Christian might attain. The lowest degree is a bare confidence that God will work faith in us. The highest is a full assurance of future glory.[9]

No affection is mentioned by Wesley as often as **love**. It is of the highest importance for Wesley. "One thing thou lackest--The love of God, without which all religion is a dead carcass." (Mark 10:21) On 1 John 4:19 Wesley writes: "We love him, because he first loved us--This is the sum of all religion, the genuine model of Christianity. None can say more: why should any one say less, or less intelligibly."[10]

The **fear** of God is a recurring theme, though Wesley is usually careful to point out that this is not a "slavish" fear.

On 1 John 4:18 he writes "A natural man has neither fear nor love, one that is awakened, fear without love; a babe in Christ, love and fear; a father in Christ, love without fear." In general, this Christian fear seems to be similar to awe, a humbling perception of God which often leads to repentance.[11]

**Joy** may be the religious affection most unlike its natural counterpart, for, as Wesley emphasizes, Christian joy is quite compatible with affliction and even sorrow. On Acts 20:19 he says "Yet joy is well consistent [with tears]. The same person may be 'sorrowful, yet always rejoicing.'"[12]

There are several concepts which might not strictly qualify as affections and yet are intimately related to them. Several, which I group together under the head of "temperance," have to do with a quality which is to accompany all of the individual affections. The other two meta-concepts - "peace" and "happiness" - are used by Wesley to represent the emotional *telos* of the entire Christian life.

As quoted in the previous chapter, "Christian **temperance** implies the voluntary abstaining from all pleasure which does not lead to God. It extends to all things inward and outward: the due government of every thought, as well as affection." (2 Peter 1:6) Having the same meaning for Wesley is "meekness": "Meekness--Holding all the affections and passions in even balance." (Gal. 5:23) "Sobriety" fits the same definition here as well: "Sobriety, in the Scripture sense, is rather the whole temper of a man, than a single virtue in him. It comprehends all that is opposite to the drowsiness of sin, the folly of ignorance, the unholiness of disorderly passions." (Titus 2:12) Passages concerning humility can also be compared here.[13]

As an over-all orientation, **peace** touches every affection. "And then the peace of God shall rule in your hearts--Shall sway every temper, affection, thought, as the reward (so the Greek word implies) of your preceding love and obedience." (Col. 3:15)  "Peace in the scriptural sense, implies all blessings, temporal and eternal." (Matt. 5:9)[14]

The couplet **happiness and holiness**, as well as the individual component words, appears in the N.T. *Notes* almost as often as the word "love."  As Albert C. Outler has pointed out[15], Wesley was a *eudaemonist*, that is, he held that the true end of the human being was happiness.  And true happiness meant happiness in God which implied "holiness," thus the constant conjunction of these terms.  He even translates "makarioi" as "happy" in the Beatitudes instead of "blessed" (as the *Philips* and *Good News* translations also do).  The "children of light" therefore are "The children of God; wise, holy, happy." (John 12:36) Likewise "So great a salvation--A deliverance from so great wickedness and misery, into so great happiness and holiness." (Heb. 2:3); and "Is for the present grievous, yet it yieldeth the peaceable fruit of righteousness--Holiness and happiness." (Heb. 12:11)  Thus, even the end of humanity is cast in terms of that which satisfies the heart most fully, that affective enjoyment of completeness:  happiness.[16]

Regarding the affections to be shunned, any affection which interferes with the *religious* affections is one that must be avoided.  Thus, the inverse of any of the above terms finds some sort of condemnation by Wesley - **intemperance, envy, despair**, etc.  **Pride** and **anger** probably find more mention than any of the others.  Pride, like its opposite, humility, can qualify every aspect of the character and thus is peculiarly vicious, while anger seems to be the prototype "passion" (as described in the last chapter) and is therefore disruptive of the whole personality.

Deserving of special notice here is **"levity."**  It may not be an affection, strictly put, but it certainly is a behavior which betrays a certain cast of the heart.  Wesley almost always condemns this for "Wherever pride, indolence, or levity revives, all the fruits of the Spirit are ready to die." (Rev. 3:2)  He even goes so far as to say that while laughter is the direct opposite of weeping, "this does not so well suit the Christian." (Rom. 12:15)   While this may seem rather extreme, it does have the virtue of specifying Christian joy and happiness.   If we see that joy and happiness do not mean levity, cleverness or mindless glee, we are prepared for the more complex, and more fulfilling, conceptions which Christianity offers.[17]

### Doctrines and Issues Shaped by Affective Language

In the N.T. *Notes*, there are many instances of a theological doctrine taking on a particular shape because of the affective language used to express it.   That is, many of Wesley's most important doctrines had to deal with the heart and its affections directly because of the central role that the affective life plays in Wesley's construal of Christianity.   Listed below are some of the more important and interesting ones each accompanied by a brief description of how they relate to the religious affections.

### The Kingdom of God

John Wesley, though he often spoke about "fleeing the wrath to come," was anything but an otherworldly, pie-in-the-sky preacher.   This is shown in his descriptions of the "Kingdom of God" in which the human heart has a peculiarly important place.   "For the kingdom of God--That is, true religion, does not consist in external observances. But in righteousness--The image of God stamped on the heart; the love of God and man, accompanied with the peace that passeth all understanding, and joy in the Holy Ghost." (Rom. 14:17)   Again, in 1 Cor. 4:20 "For the kingdom of God--Real religion does not consist in words, but in the power of God ruling the heart."[18]

## Soteriology and Pneumatology

As was seen above, the Holy Spirit's connection to the human heart is very close, though not so close as to rule out human freedom and agency, even in the production of the religious affections. As we see in Wesley's comment on Matt. 1:16, the affections are also peculiarly tied to the work of the second person of the Trinity:

> We are by nature at a distance from God, alienated from Him, and incapable of a free access to Him. Hence we want a mediator, an intercessor; in a word, a Christ in his priestly office. This regards our state with respect to God. And with respect to ourselves, we find a total darkness, blindness, ignorance of God, and the things of God. Now here we want Christ in His prophetic office, to enlighten our minds, and teach us the whole will of God. We also find within us a strange misrule of appetites and passions. For these we want Christ in His royal character, to reign in our hearts, and subdue all things to Himself.

Related to this are the themes of sanctification, perfection, and assurance, all of which find ample expression in terms of the affections in the N.T. *Notes*.[19]

## The Passibility of God

Of particular theological interest is the fact that, despite his emphasis on the affections of the human, Wesley, in the classical tradition, is uneasy about attributing passibility to God. On Luke 15:7, which speaks about the joy in heaven, Wesley says "Yea, and God Himself so readily forgives and receives them, that He may be *represented* as having part in the joy." (emphasis mine)

Where Heb. 4:10 quotes Psalm 95 which says that God "was grieved," Wesley inserts "to speak after the manner of men."

Wesley does often speak about the love which God has, though (e.g., 1 John 4:8, John 4:24), and he explains how this is consistent with God's nature in his comment on Rom. 5:9:

> By his blood--By His bloodshedding. We shall be saved from the wrath through him--That is, from all the effects of the wrath of God. But is there then wrath in God? Is not wrath a human passion? And how can this human passion be in God? We may answer this by another question: Is not love a human passion? And how can this human passion be in God? But to answer directly: wrath in man, and so love in man, is a human passion. But wrath in God is not a human passion; nor is love, as it is in God. Therefore the inspired writers ascribe both the one and the other to God only in an analogical sense.

His use of the pejorative term "passion" here might be taken to show that he is trying to distinguish between natural and religious affections.[20]

### Ecclesiology

Though Wesley had many scathing remarks to make about the outward Christian, the "outward-court worshipers" (Rev.13:15) who had no inner religion, he also made many references to the importance of church life for the believer: "And where can we expect this sacred effusion, but in a humble attendance on divine appointments." (Matt. 3:16) Similarly, he warned "Enthusiasts, observe this! Expect no end without the means." (1 Tim. 4:13)[21]

Interestingly, he discusses "schism" - a topic he obviously had to deal with often as he tried to hold the

Methodists within the Church of England - only in terms of wrong affections or tempers. On 1 Cor. 1:10 he says "And that there be no schisms among you--No alienation of affection from each other. Is this word ever taken in any other sense in Scripture? But that ye be joined in the same mind--Affections, desires. And judgment--Touching all the grand truths of the gospel." Later in the same book, he elaborates:

> Therefore, the indulging any temper contrary to this tender care of each other is the true scriptural schism. This is, therefore, a quite different thing from the orderly separation from corrupt churches which later ages have stigmatized as schisms; and have made a pretence for the vilest cruelties, oppressions, and murders, that have troubled the Christian world. (1 Cor. 11:18)

**Prayer**

Given Wesley's emphasis on the affections, it is no surprise to see that

> We do not pray to inform God of our wants....The chief thing wanting is, a fit disposition on our part to receive His grace and blessing. Consequently, one great office of prayer is, to produce such a disposition in us, to exercise our dependence on God, to increase our desire of the things we ask for, to make us so sensible of our wants, that we may never cease wrestling till we have prevailed for the blessing. (Matt. 6:8)

Throughout the N.T. *Notes*, there are many references to prayer as the language of the heart.[22]

## Sex Role Differences

Of particular contemporary interest are the remarks which Wesley made regarding the differences between man and woman on the question of the affections. The fullest statement on this theme is found in his comment on Acts 17:4:

> Our freethinkers pique themselves upon observing that women are more religious than men; and this, in compliment both to religion and good manners, they impute to the weakness of their understandings. And, indeed, as far as nature can go in imitating religion by performing the outward acts of it, this picture of religion may make a fairer show in women than in men, both by reason of their more tender passions, and their modesty, which will make those actions appear to more advantage. But in the case of true religion, which always implies taking up the cross, especially in time of persecution, women lie naturally under a great disadvantage, as having less courage than men. So that their embracing the gospel was a stronger evidence of the power of Him whose strength is perfected in weakness, as a stronger assistance of the Holy Spirit was needful for them to overcome their natural fearfulness.

Today we would not attribute to women the "natural" characteristics which either the "freethinkers" ("weak understandings") or Wesley ("fearfulness") assigned to women. Most today would allow that men and women have varying amounts of these virtues and vices depending more on their individual endowments and histories rather than on the basis of their gender. Note, however, that the crucial point made in this passage is that it is *second* nature (that which the Spirit forms in us) which is crucial for determining true *Christian* nature. What we may or may not start with in the process of becoming a Christian (our "first" nature we might say) is less important than the perfecting possibilities of the Spirit. Wesley's sexism at this point does no violence to the principle thrust of his affection-related theology.

Regardless of whether such differences are "natural" or otherwise, though, Wesley recognized that the different ways men and women are expected to behave calls for some specific tailoring of the Christian message. On Eph. 6:2,4 he says "Honour--That is, love, reverence, obey, assist, in all things. The mother is particularly mentioned, as being more liable to be slighted than the father....And ye, fathers--Mothers are included; but fathers are named, as being more apt to be stern and severe."

It should be noted, though, that he was not entirely a man of his age on the issue of sexism. Though he was implicitly loyal to the Word of God as found in the Scriptures, he felt compelled to add a qualifying phrase to the famous passage of 1 Cor. 14:34: "Let your women be silent in the churches--Unless they are under an extraordinary impulse of the Spirit." This hardly rescues him from the ranks of male chauvinism, but it does, to some extent, reflect the fact that the role of women in Methodism was much more important than it was in the Church of England.[23]

### Conclusion: The Affections in the N.T. *Notes*

We can now see that, for Wesley, true religion, the inward kingdom of the heart's affections, was no head-long plunge into subjectivity, but a reasoned attention to the things of God which leads us gently toward Christian works and away from sin. No complete mastery of the inner depths is either implied nor necessary in Wesley's emphasis on the affections. Wesley never denied the fundamental mysteriousness of human nature. In fact he explicitly says on Rom. 9:3 that "Human words cannot fully describe the motions of souls that are full of God."[24]

What he was sure of, though, is that Christianity can address and sanctify the emotional life of the believer. In fact, it must do this if it is truly to be Christianity. Let us turn now to Wesley's other writings to see how this theme is picked up and elaborated upon in the various contexts of his sermons, letters, journal and abridgements.

1. Cf. Mark 3:30 and Luke 12:10.

2. See G.D. Marshall's "On Being Affected" in *Mind*, volume 77, April, 1968, 243-259, for a contemporary philosopher's differentiation between an emotion's cause, occasion and object. In addition to the object, the person's history is also part of the causal nexus of an emotion since having an emotion entails the simultaneous awareness of the object and the self. This is also how we are both passive and active in an emotion. The object makes us passive to some extent by bringing its own nature to the experience, but we are active in attending to the object and interpreting the object in the light of our own history.

3. Many modern philosophers have specifically drawn attention to the dispositional nature of the emotions. See, for example, Gilbert Ryle's *The Concept of Mind* (New York: Harper and Row, 1949) especially chapters 4 and 5.

4. On this theme of relating to our neighbors through God compare Augustine's *On Christian Doctrine*, Book One, section 32: "The greatest reward is that we enjoy Him and that all of us who enjoy Him may enjoy one another in Him."

5. See Rex Matthews' paper, cited in note 13, page 65 above.

6. Here is one example where looking at the original Greek of the text can be of benefit. Where Romans 12:16 reads "agree in the same affection toward each other" and Colossians 3:2 says "Set your affections on the things above", the Greek in both cases uses a word that could be translated as "Mind ye" (phronountes; phroneite).

7. Wesley's difference from someone like Schleiermacher could

not be any clearer than on this point. See section 3 of *The Christian Faith* where Schleiermacher states that true piety is neither a knowing or a doing but a feeling, an immediate self-consciousness.

8. See also 1 Tim. 6:11, 1 Cor. 7:19, Matt. 20:23, Matt. 25:3, John 4:14. All references here and below are not to the Scripture texts themselves, but Wesley's comments on these texts.

9. See also 1 Tim. 1:1, Eph. 4:4.

10. To list just a fraction of the other references to love: Luke 10:28, 1 John 4:8, John 10:27, John 3:36, Mark 12:33, Eph. 3:17.

11. Cf. 2 Cor. 11:3, Jude 1:15, 2 Cor. 7:1 on fear. On repentance and other personality requirements for belief, see Acts 26:20, Acts 28:26, Acts 22:19, Acts 20:21, 1 Peter 4:11, 1 Tim. 6:4, etc.

12. See Rev. 3:8, 1 Cor. 7:30, Luke 15:23, Matt. 4:23, etc.

13. Cf. Luke 15:12, Matt. 23:12.

14. See also 1 Thess. 5:23, Phil. 4:7, John 20:21, etc.

15. *Theology in the Wesleyan Spirit* (Nashville: Discipleship Resources, 1975) 81.

16. Just a few of the references to happiness and holiness: 1 John (intro.), Matt. 6:10, Matt. 5:3, Matt. 5:12, Matt. 5:48, 1 Cor. 15:31.

17. Other references to the vicious affections: Eph. 5:4, 1 Peter 3:12, James 4:5, Mark 7:22, Mark 9:38, Rom. 1:29, Matt. 23:25.

18. See also Luke 17:21, Matt. 13:31, Luke 1:32, Luke 11:52, John 3:3, Matt. 23:31.

19. On Christology, see John 1:14, Heb. 2:10, Heb. 8:12. See also John Deschner's *Wesley's Christology* (Dallas: S.M.U. Press, 1985) and my critique of it in Chapter 7, below. On sanctification see 1 Thess. 4:3, Matthew 5:7, Phil. 3:13. On assurance see 1 Cor. 12:3, 1 Thess. 1:5, Heb. 6:11.

20. Christ's sufferings on the cross were real enough for Wesley, though, so he was definitely no Docetic. See his notes to Matt. 26:37 and Matt. 27:34.

21. On the sacraments and ecclesiology and their implications for the affections, see John 20:23, Acts 2:42, Matt. 12:7, Eph. 5:26.

22. See, for example, Matt. 6:7, 1 Tim. 2:1, 1 Tim. 4:15, Luke 11:1.

23. See Paul Chilcote's "The Women Pioneers of Early Methodism" in *Wesleyan Theology Today* (Nashville: Kingswood Books, 1985), 180-184.

24. That the depths of our felt life remain mysterious even to those who are  thought of as "experts" in the area can be seen in Kierkegaard's *Concluding Unscientific Postscript* where he says "For feeling is like the river Niger in Africa: its source is not known, nor its outlet, but only its course." (Princeton: Princeton University Press, 1941) 212.

# CHAPTER FIVE

## The Word Proclaimed: True Religion and its Counterfeit as Seen in Wesley's Sermons

I think a preacher or a writer of Sermons has lost his way when he imitates any of the French orators....Only let his language be plain, proper and clear, and it is enough. God himself has told us how to speak, both as to the matter and the manner: "If any man speak," in the name of God, "let him speak as the oracles of God;" and if he would imitate any part of these above the rest, let it be the First Epistle of St. John. This is the style, the most excellent style, for every gospel preacher. And let him aim at no more ornament than he finds in that sentence, which is the sum of the whole gospel, "We love Him, because He first loved us."

Preface to *Sermons on Several Occasions*

Giving an exhaustive account of Wesley's remarks about the affections in his sermons could be a book unto itself, just as our study of the affections in his Biblical *Notes* could have expanded into an independent study. Because of what has been established in the previous chapters, however, we need not begin our present inquiry as if we were starting *ex nihilo* on the subject of Wesley's views about emotion. We have seen in both the O.T. *Notes* and the N.T. *Notes* that the affections are central for Wesley.

The evidence accumulated so far, in fact, would cause us to be extremely surprised if the affections were not a part of the basic fabric of the sermons. As it turns out, no such surprise will be forthcoming; Christianity and the religious affections are as inseparable in the sermons as they were in the *Notes*. The conceptual distinctions concerning the affections which we have already established (e.g., the rational nature of the heart, the transitive and dispositional nature of the affections, etc.) are also to be found in the sermons. Let us assume, then, familiarity with the basic thrust of his affectional conception of Christianity in order to see how this is expressed in the fuller narrative context of a sermon.

Not all 151 sermons, of course, will be directly pertinent to our task, just as not every text of Scripture elicited a comment about the affections from Wesley in his biblical commentaries. I do claim, however, that the generalizations about the affections which I will make below based on selected passages are, on the whole, consistent with the entire sermon corpus. My comments are not exhaustive but they are representative.

## The Sermons as a Whole

Albert Outler has claimed that Wesley's theological career can be divided into three different periods: pre-1738, 1738-1765 and 1765-1791[1], though he is careful to point-out that the sermons from the early period contain the seeds of his later emphases, and that even the last sermons written display the same intent of their predecessors.[2] This is consistent with Wesley's famous remark found in his *Journal* for September 1, 1778. There he stated "Forty years ago I knew and preached every Christian doctrine which I preach now."[3] With a few important exceptions, noted below, the changes in the content of Wesley's sermons are of emphasis and refinement, not basic thrust.

When considering Wesley's sermons, though, we must keep in mind an important distinction between the sermons that we have in written form and those sermons which Wesley preached. Richard Heitzenrater reports that of the 131 sermons Wesley published in his lifetime, it is likely that only 15 were preached in the form they were published.[4] Also, many of Wesley's favorite texts for oral preaching never appeared on the printed page. Frank Baker states, for example, that a sermon on Mark 12:34 was preached 51 times according to Wesley's records, but it was never published. Similarly, sermons on I Kings 18:21 and II Kings 5:12 were preached 38 and 19 times respectively, yet neither was ever published.[5]

On the other hand, the sermon "Catholic Spirit" (on II Kings 10:15) was published though only preached twice. The published sermons were, therefore, "deliberately prepared as a body of preached doctrine rather than a collection of favourite sermons."[6] Though the oral sermons were longer and more anecdotal, the doctrinal substance of the two genres was apparently consistent.[7]

## Wesley's Own View of the Sermons

Outler has claimed that all of the sermons will be misread "unless they are understood as experimental statements and restatements of [Wesley's] vision of the Christian life."[8] Since the Christian life is Wesley's focus, it is not surprising to see that soteriology is his primary doctrinal interest.[9] What God has done and is doing for us is never far removed from Wesley's preaching, and all talk about creation, sin, eschatology, the church or any of the other traditional doctrinal loci receive Wesley's attention only as they are relevant to our present concrete existence. All of this can be seen in Wesley's Preface to his *Sermons on Several Occasions*.

Wesley reproduced the same Preface in every edition of his sermons which appeared in his lifetime from 1746 to 1787.[10] In it he made many comments similar to those he made in the Preface to his N.T. *Notes*. For instance, his role as a folk theologian is seen when he says "...I now write (as I generally speak) *ad populum* - to the bulk of mankind - to those who neither relish nor understand the art of speaking, but who notwithstanding are competent judges of those truths which are necessary to present and future happiness."[11] He also reasserts the biblical foundation of his thought by repeating his famous subjunctive: "Let me be *homo unius libri*."[12]

He wastes little time broaching the topic of the affections in the Preface. He says that in these sermons he has "endeavored to describe the true, the scriptural, experimental religion."[13] He continues that it was especially his desire

> first, to guard those who are just setting their faces toward heaven (and who, having little acquaintance with the things of God, are the more liable to be turned out of the way) from formality, from mere outside religion, which has almost driven heart-religion out of the world; and secondly, to warn those who know the religion of the heart, the faith which worketh by love, lest at any time they make void the law through faith, and so fall back into the snare of the devil.[14]

Shortly after this, he brings up both a crucial Christian affection - love - and an important negative affection - anger - in the context of challenging his critics for correction instead of sheer *animus*:

> For God's sake, if it be possible to avoid it let us not provoke one another to wrath. Let us not kindle in

each other this fire of hell, much less blow it up into a flame. If we could discern truth by that dreadful light, would it not be loss rather than gain? For how far is love, even with many wrong opinions, to be preferred before truth itself without love? We may die without the knowledge of many truths and yet be carried into Abraham's bosom. But if we die without love, what will knowledge avail? Just as much as it avails the devil and his angels!

The God of love forbid we should ever make the trial! May he prepare us for the knowledge of all truth, by filling our hearts with all his love, and with all joy and peace in believing.[15]

Already in the Preface, then, we see the themes of happiness, inward heart-religion, love, and warnings against self-deception and anger. But this Preface is affixed to the sermons Wesley published in his lifetime. Before we consider these sermons, let us step back to consider those early sermons which received their first publication in volume four of Abingdon Press's edition of Wesley's *Works*. Here we can see many affectional themes take their first form.

### The Early Unpublished Sermons[16]

Even the first of these sermons, on Job 3:17 and inscribed in John Wesley's hand "The first sermon I ever wrote," contains his lifelong emphasis on the central role of the affectional life for the Christian. After mentioning happiness several times in the first paragraphs of the sermon, he eventually states "The desire of happiness is inseparably [bound] to our nature, and is the spring which sets all our faculties a-moving." (#133, 209)[17] The happiness of the saints shall be even greater in heaven "When God shall make them possess the fullness of joy at his own right hand for evermore, and drink of the rivers of pleasure in the new Jerusalem." (#133, 213)

This theme of pleasure, and its qualified relationship to happiness which we saw in the N.T. *Notes*, is found in two other of the early sermons. In number 142 "The Wisdom of Winning Souls," Wesley says "He is to be convinced that religion forbids no pleasure but what would deprive him of a greater, nor requires any pain to be embraced, unless in order to more than equal pleasure." (#142, 312) Similar is number 145:

> Therefore whenever you have wholly renounced yourself, i.e., when you do nothing as or because you will, then you will be perfectly happy. When once you seek your own pleasure in nothing, you shall find it in everything. Therefore think not at all, what is or is not pleasing to yourself: this is wide [of the mark]. But simply whether this be pleasing to God. (350)

The transitive nature of the affections is shown clearly in number 134 "Seek ye First the Kingdom of God." Wesley says that it is impossible to serve two masters (our temporal and eternal interests) at once, because "...the affections [are] not ... capable of fixing at the same time on two so different objects..." (#134, 217) Later in this same sermon, Wesley shows just what such a quest for the kingdom will entail. Will it entail insuperable difficulties? "Nay, 'what doth the Lord require of thee but to do justly, and to love mercy, and to walk humbly with thy God.' What doth he require of thee but those previous dispositions of mind which are absolutely necessary to qualify thee for the enjoyment either of present or future happiness?" (223)

In fragment 138C "On Dissimulation," we see that the "most inexcusable" dissimulation is that "which counterfeits affection where there is none; or where there is, couples it with dissembling." (263) Aside from its inherent wrongness, such deception leads to "the most low and abject slavery" since if the person is to carry off the ruse

> He must submit to perform all the tender offices that naturally flow from real affection, all which nothing but real affection can make pleasing. To perform them on any other principle is at best a dull, insipid task, commonly wearisome and painful. (264-5)

Here is a concise picture of the importance of the affections for Christianity ("most inexcusable...") as well as the fact that the Christian affections are dispositions from which Christian actions "naturally flow."

In sermon number 139 "On the Sabbath" we see that achieving certain affections is an important goal for Christians and that securing the means to produce them are to be a determinative element in our ethics. "Some recreation is therefore allowed on this day [the Sabbath], because few minds are of so firm a temper as to be able to preserve a cheerful devotion, a lively gratitude, without it. It is therefore a proper work of necessity so far as it conduces to these ends." (276)

In two of these early sermons, number 141 "The Image of God" and number 146 "The One Thing Needful," a particular configuration of the affections is definitive of humanity both before and after the Fall. The sanctified human who, because of Christ's atonement, once again is in the image of God, is also characterized, in part, by the affections of his will. In the pre-Fall state, humanity not only had an understanding which could distinguish truth from falsehood, but was also possessed of a "far greater and nobler" endowment, namely, a perfect will:

> It could not but be perfect while it followed the dictates of such an understanding. His affections were rational, even, and regular--if we may be allowed to say

"affections," for properly speaking he had but one: man
was what God is, Love. Love filled the whole
expansion of his soul; it possessed him without a rival.
Every movement of his heart was love: it knew no
other fervour. Love was his vital heat; it was the genial
warmth that animated his whole frame. (#141, 294-
5)[18]

When the perfect understanding and will were joined with
liberty only happiness resulted. (295)

After the Fall, however, the understanding could
mistake falsehood for truth, and truth for falsehood, and
the will, accordingly, was "seized by legions of vile
affections. Grief and anger and hatred and fear and shame,
at once rushed in upon it; the whole train of earthly,
sensual, and devilish passions fastened on and tore it in
pieces." (298)  Not only did the earthly affections gain
ascendancy, but

love itself, that ray of the Godhead, that balm of life,
now became a torment. Its light being gone, it
wandered about seeking rest and finding none; till at
length, equally unable to subsist without any and to
feel out its proper object, it reclined itself upon the
painted trifles, the gilded poison of earthly enjoyments.
(298)

Of course, because of this, freedom vanished and thus went
happiness. (298-9)

Wesley's answer to the question of how we are to
escape such a predicament shows signs of the will-mysticism
of Law and Taylor which still held sway over him in his early
years,[19] and this is one of the noteworthy differences
between these early sermons and his later ones.  Instead of
answering  resoundingly "by grace through faith" as he
would so often after Aldersgate, here, though referring to

Christ, the emphasis is on human action. Participating in the death of Christ will be those "who accept of the means which he hath prepared, who walk by the rules which he hath given them." (299) The first step to this glorious change is humility. The understanding, "thus enlightened by humility, immediately directs us to reform our will by charity." (300)

Though grace seems to be downplayed in favor of human self-discipline, the end of the process is the same in this early stage of his career as it was at the end of his life: to root-out of our souls all "unmanly passions" such as malice, uncleanness, intemperance and wrath and reforming our love. Wesley describes it as a process of collecting "the scattered beams of that affection which is truly human, truly divine, and fix them on that Sovereign Good 'in whom we live, move, and have our being'..." (300) Becoming kind and forgiving to one another completes the process and thus knowledge, virtue, freedom and happiness will all be restored. (300)

This renewal of the fallen nature is the "One Thing Needful" of sermon 146 and the same themes run throughout. The devil binds us with "vile affections," "unholy passions" and "diabolical tempers." (354) But love gives us perfect freedom from these (355), our "renewal in the love of God" (356) restores the image lost in the Fall.[20]

Implied in much of the above is an intimate connection between the affections and the understanding, and this theme receives direct treatment in sermon number 142 "The Wisdom of Winning Souls." There he says that after a person is both convinced and confirmed in the knowledge of the truth, that is, after his understanding has been strengthened, then

> 'tis time to use the other great means of winning souls, namely, the regulating his affections. Indeed without doing this the other can't be done throughly; he that

would well enlighten the head must cleanse the heart. Otherwise the disorder of the will again disorders the understanding; and perverseness of affection will again cause an equal perverseness of judgment. For whatever inclination is contrary to reason is likewise destructive of it; and whoever makes the world his god, that god will surely blind his eyes. (313)

It is not, then, a one-way flow from the understanding to the affections. Certain affections must be present, and others absent, if the Gospel is truly to be the ruling principle of our lives. There are, in short, personality requirements (not just doctrinal and intellectual requirements) for mature Christianity. These personality requirements are none other than the religious affections.

The all-importance of one particular affection is seen in sermon number 144 "The Love of God." Taking Mark 12:30 ("Thou shalt love the Lord thy God with all thy heart, and with all thy soul, and with all thy mind, and with all thy strength") as his text, Wesley makes several now-familiar points. Among these are: that only love can perfect human happiness (331); that we are to love the Creator more than the creature (331 and 340ff.); that love of neighbor flows from love of God (335); and that the affection from which an action flows determines the worth of the action (341-2). As much of the sermon is spent in attacking faulty notions of what love is, the whole sermon can also be seen as another effort at preventing affectional delusions from arising in his audience.

Even in these early sermons we can see that Wesley has no taste for explaining in detail how the Spirit works with the believer to create the affections, only that it does in fact happen. "But how he worketh this in us, who shall tell? Who shall point out his particular methods of working? This indeed we know, that when the passions are laid, and our souls are calm and still, then chiefly the Spirit of God loves to move upon the face of the waters; yet are we not able to explain how he moves." (#140, 284)

Wesley knew both early and late in his career that if we keep our eyes fixed on God, His Holy Spirit will dwell in us and

> He shall purify your hearts by faith from every earthly thought, every unholy affection. He shall establish your souls with so lively a hope as already lays hold on the prize of your high calling. He shall fill you with peace, and joy, and love! Love, the brightness of his glory, the express image of his person. Love which never rests, never faileth, but still spreads its flame, still goeth on conquering and to conquer, till what was but a weak, foolish, wavering, sinful creature, be filled with all the fullness of God! (#148, 377)

That this sermon was written over two years before his famous experience at Aldersgate shows that there was more continuity to Wesley's conceptions than is often thought. Let us now turn to those sermons which were published and which express his mature views on all matters he held to be most important.

## The Published Sermons

Though certain sermons have been designated as doctrinal standards for the "people called Methodists" there is no reason for us to restrict our analysis to these only. Wesley put his name to well over one hundred published sermons and in doing so claimed the thought contained therein to be worthy of reflection. The ideas expressed in those sermons published after the so-called "standards" do no violence to his previously published views, and in fact they usually help to supplement and clarify his previously expressed convictions.

As a result of my research, I have isolated four major themes in the sermon corpus which are both centrally important to Wesley's theology and rich in references to the affections. Examining these themes will show us how Wesley was compelled to speak about the affections when elaborating the core of the Gospel. These themes are: The Nature of Christianity; The Assurance of Faith; Sin, the Believer and Perfection; and Works and the Heart. Let us consider first Wesley's answer to that most basic and over-arching question: What is Christianity?

## What Christianity is, and What it is Not

The first sermon in the extant published corpus of Wesley's sermons is "Salvation by Faith" and by putting it first, Wesley was making a clear statement that the will-mysticism of Law, Taylor and Kempis, while useful, was not sufficient to salvation. He had rediscovered, both in his Aldersgate experience and in his studies of the *Homilies* and "Articles of Religion" of his church, that it is grace through *faith* which justifies us. The whole sermon is an exposition of what this faith is.

First of all, Wesley wants to make clear that it is "by grace" through faith that we are saved. "Grace is the source, faith the condition, of salvation." (#1, 118) As with all of his mature thought, grace is everywhere, although it is by no means irresistible.

But more specifically, what manner of faith is under discussion here? First of all, it is not the "faith of a heathen." Such a faith entailed believing in "the being and attributes of God, a future state of reward and punishment, and the obligatory nature of moral virtue." (#1, 119)

Secondly, Christian faith is not the faith of a devil. Such faith assents to what the heathen believes but in addition, the devil knows that "Jesus is the Son of God, the Christ and the Saviour of the World." (*Ibid.*) Christian faith is neither (thirdly) that which the apostles had while Christ was on earth, for the power of his death and resurrection was not yet available. So what is the Christian faith?

> It may be answered: first, in general, it is faith in Christ--Christ, and God through Christ, are the proper object of it. Herein therefore it is fully distinguished by this--it is not barely a speculative, rational thing, a cold, lifeless assent, a train of ideas in the head; but also a disposition of the heart. For thus saith the Scripture, 'With the heart man believeth unto righteousness.' And, 'If thou shalt confess with thy mouth the Lord Jesus, and shalt believe with thy *heart* that God hath raised him from the dead, thou shalt be saved.' [emphasis his] (#1, 120)

In further explaining this, he says that such faith saves us from guilt and fear, though "Not indeed from a filial fear of offending, but from all servile fear..." (#1, 122) Likewise, such faith gives peace and leads to rejoicing "in hope of the glory of God....And the love of God is shed abroad in their hearts through the Holy Ghost which is given unto them." (#1, 123) Finally, those who truly believe will use all of the ordinances, do good works and "enjoy and manifest all holy and heavenly tempers, even the same 'mind that was in Christ Jesus'." (#1, 125)

This same structure of alternately describing what a Christian is *not*, then what a Christian *is*, can also be found in sermon number 2 "The Almost Christian." The almost Christian has honesty, truth, justice, and love as well, though only a love "that would not prejudice oneself." Such people even have "A form of godliness" though it is only "the *outside* of a real Christian." [emphasis his] (#2, 131-2) But beyond this, the almost Christian can even have "sincerity," a "real, inward principle of religion from whence these outward actions flow." (#2, 134)

But what, then, is implied in being "altogether a Christian?" Nothing other than the love of God, the love of our neighbor, the faith which purifies the heart and yields repentance and good works. He sums this up at the close of the sermon by saying:

> May we all thus experience what it is to be not almost only, but altogether Christians! Being justified freely by his grace, through the redemption that is in Jesus, knowing we have peace with God through Jesus Christ, rejoicing in hope of the glory of God, and having the love of God shed abroad in our hearts by the Holy Ghost given unto us! (#2, 141)

Denying that faith-as-assent is *by itself* enough to make one a Christian is found throughout the sermons and this can be seen as the obverse of his emphasis on the affections. Compare sermon number 4 "Scriptural Christianity": "'Christianity'; not as it implies a set of opinions, a system of doctrines, but as it refers to men's hearts and lives." (161); and number 7 "The Way to the Kingdom": "He may assent to all the three creeds...and yet 'tis possible he may have no religion at all, no more than a Jew, Turk, or Pagan." (220); and number 62 "The End of Christ's Coming": "and least of all dream that orthodoxy, right opinion, (vulgarly called *faith*) is religion. Of all religious dreams, this is the vainest; which takes hay and stubble for gold tried in the fire!...Take no less for his religion, than the 'faith that worketh by love;' all inward and outward holiness." (483); and, finally, number 130 "On Living Without God":

> I believe the merciful God regards the lives and tempers of men more than their ideas. I believe he respects the goodness of the heart, rather than the clearness of the head; and that if the heart of a man be filled (by the grace of God, and the power of his Spirit)

with the humble, gentle, patient love of God and man, God will not cast him into everlasting fire, prepared for the devil and his angels, because his ideas are not clear, or because his conceptions are confused. 'Without holiness,' I own, 'no man shall see the Lord;' but I dare not add, 'or clear ideas.' (175)

Related to this is Wesley's assertion that we should let reason do all that it is capable of and not undervalue it, but neither should we overvalue it. For we must acknowledge that reason is "utterly incapable of giving either faith, or hope or love; and, consequently, of producing either real virtue, or substantial happiness. Expect these from a higher source, even from the Father of the spirits of all flesh." (#70, 600)

As seen in this last passage, Wesley's stress on happiness and holiness as the marks of the Christian life is present in these published sermons as it was in the *Notes*. Indeed, Outler mentions in a note in his Introduction to the sermons that the correlation of happiness and holiness appears in no less than 30 of Wesley's sermons. (35, note 28) It is even used negatively in number 78 "Spiritual Idolatry" where we are told that the best way to keep ourselves from idols is to "be deeply convinced that none of them bring happiness." (111)

This whole problem of idolatry and self-deception is dealt with at length in number 37 "The Nature of Enthusiasm." Here Wesley says that if one performs a round of outward duties, asserts orthodox opinions and exhibits a certain quantity of "heathen morality" then people will consider such a person within the bounds of acceptability. "But if you aim at the religion of the heart, if you talk of 'righteousness, and peace, and joy in the Holy Ghost', then it will not be long before your sentence is passed, "Thou art beside thyself." (46) But it was so important to attain to this "righteousness, peace and joy" that Wesley ran the risk of being called an enthusiast and in this sermon he set out his own counter-attacking notion of what enthusiasm really is.

The part of this sermon most pertinent to our concern with the affections is the passage where he speaks about knowing the will of God. How are we to know this?

> Not by waiting for supernatural dreams; not by expecting God to reveal it in visions; not by looking for any *particular impressions* [emphasis his] or sudden impulses on his mind: no; but by consulting the oracles of God. 'To the law and to the testimony!' This is the general method of knowing what is 'the holy and acceptable will of God.' (54)

Here we again see, as we previously noted in our discussion of his N.T. *Notes*, Wesley warning against a retreat to subjectivity for guidance in our spiritual life. In the sermons, Wesley emphasizes the more holistic "affections" over against the narrow awareness-of-sensation that we associate with the term "feeling." (For other references to objective, external, checks on our spiritual life, see number 65 "The Duty of Reproving Our Neighbor." On humility and repentance as checks on our emotions, see number 48 "Self-Denial.")

We can see, then, that in the sermons, the affectional nature of Christianity is clear. Let us now move on to consider the question of the nature of assurance. Here we will find the complex issue of the relation of the religious affections to the Holy Spirit again addressed.

### The Assurance of Faith

The sensitive inter-play between our spirit and the Holy Spirit in the affections of the believer which we discerned in the *Notes* is again seen in the sermons. My interpretation of the *Notes* on this topic (that the Spirit is active, yet not in an overpowering way) is confirmed by Outler's Introduction where he says that on Wesley's terms, the believer is "indwelt and led by the Spirit within rather than being possessed by the Spirit as if by some irresistible force." (75)  The implications of this for the religious affections are seen especially in three sermons:  "The Witness of the Spirit I," "The Witness of the Spirit II" and "The Witness of Our Own Spirit."

The first two of these sermons (both on Romans 8:16) were written over twenty years apart, yet both have the same goal in mind, namely, to show the enthusiasts how they "have mistaken the voice of their own imagination for this 'witness of the Spirit' of God, and thence idly presumed they were the children of God while they were doing the works of the devil!" (#10, 269)  As usual, Wesley declined to specify *how* this assurance is worked in us (276) - he offers no schematic of our spiritual plumbing.  Nonetheless, he maintains that there are several important conceptual clarifications that can and should be made.

The most important point Wesley makes in these sermons is that there *is* a direct witness of the Spirit, but it never appears *without* its fruits which are, of course, the religious affections of peace, joy, love, etc. (see Galatians 5:22-23 which Wesley quotes or alludes to on pages 279, 283, 286, 297).  One determines if one has this assuring witness, therefore, not by waiting for some Damascus road experience (though Wesley would never deny that such do in fact occur), but by determining if one loves God:

> He that now loves God--that delights and rejoices in him with an humble joy, an holy delight, and an obedient love--is a child of God;
>> But I thus love, delight, and rejoice in God;
>> Therefore I am a child of God;

then a Christian can in no wise doubt of his being a child of God. (#10, 276)

In the later sermon he makes the same point: "When our spirit is conscious of this--of love, joy, peace, long-suffering, gentleness, goodness--it easily infers from these premises that we are the children of God." (#11, 289)  In countering an objection to this, he also shows that "experience" has a limited role to play in determining the core of the Gospel:

> It is objected, first, 'Experience is not sufficient to prove a doctrine which is not founded on Scripture.' This is undoubtedly true, and it is an important truth. But it does not affect the present question, for it has been shown that this doctrine is founded on Scripture. Therefore experience is properly alleged to confirm it. (#11, 293)

As always, the Bible is the final authority.  "Experience" can not by itself "prove" something relating to the Faith which is unscriptural.

In summarizing this theme, Wesley draws two inferences.  The first is "let none ever presume to rest in any supposed testimony of the Spirit which is separate from the fruit of it." (#11, 297)  The second is "Let none rest in any supposed fruit of the Spirit without the witness." (298)  As he had said earlier,

> ...to secure us from all delusion, God gives us two witnesses that we are his children.  And this they testify conjointly.  Therefore, 'what God hath joined together, let not man put asunder.' (295)

The third sermon in this series, number 12 "The Witness of Our Own Spirit," takes 2 Corinthians 1:12 as its text: "This is our rejoicing, the testimony of our conscience, that in simplicity and godly sincerity, not with fleshly wisdom, but by the grace of God, we have had our conversation in the world." The sermon, then, is "to show what is the nature and ground of a Christian's joy. We know, in general, it is that happy peace, that calm satisfaction of spirit, which arises from such a testimony of his conscience as is here described by the Apostle." (#12, 300)

Here we are thrown back to the language of "conscience" which we also encountered in the *Notes*, and, as in the *Notes*, Wesley at first appears to be proposing some universal principle present in all: "we may understand by conscience a faculty or power, implanted by God in every soul that comes into the world, of perceiving what is right or wrong in his own heart or life, in his tempers, thoughts, words, and actions." (#12, 302) But here, as in the *Notes*, he qualifies this by saying that the conscience is determined by the "rule" which controls it, and this "rule" is quite different for Christians than the rule of the world. (302) (Compare also 310 where Wesley shows that Christian joy is not a natural joy.) Here again we can see his absolute rejection of a naturalistic and autonomous ethical sense as proposed by Shaftesbury and Hutcheson while at the same time he asserts that the testimony of a good conscience *is* part of his vision of the Christian life. These same themes are elaborated in sermon 105 "On Conscience."

The witness of our own spirit, then, is not an experience available to anyone, but only to *Christians* who have been formed in the Christian "rule" of the Gospel, found in Scripture. (302-303) If we are thusly formed, "If therefore this eye of thy soul be single, all thy actions and conversation shall be 'full of light', of the light of heaven, of love and peace and joy in the Holy Ghost." (306-307) This testimony or assurance, then, is not some necessary religious *a priori* to be mystically intuited; it is the contingent result of our taking as the object of our affections God and what God has done for us:

> We are then simple of heart when the eye of our mind is singly fixed on God; when in all things we aim at God alone, as our God, our portion, our strength, our happiness, our exceeding great reward, our all in time and eternity. This is simplicity: when a steady view, a single intention of promoting his glory, of doing and suffering his blessed will, runs through our whole soul, fills all our heart, and is the constant spring of all our thoughts, desires, and purposes. (#12, 307)[21]

One last point needs to be made concerning Wesley's normative pronouncements about the Spirit and our affections. In sermon number 3 "Awake Thou That Sleepest," written by Charles Wesley, there is a rather bold claim made for either a clear and full assurance or none at all. In Outler's note to this he points out that "both brothers rather quickly modified this all-or-nothing emphasis by allowing for degrees of assurance." [Outler refers here to John's letter of March 28, 1768 to Dr. Rutherford, and sermons 89, 106, and 117.] (154n) The mature position of Wesley regarding the stages of growth in faith is best represented by his distinction (seen already in our discussion of the *Notes*) between the "faith of a servant" (characterized primarily by *fear* of God) and the "faith of a son" (characterized primarily by *love* of God). See #9 "The Spirit of Bondage and Adoption" (and especially Outler's note on 250).

Of interest also is the conversation between Melville Horne and John Wesley which took place around 1789 which Outler also quotes. The germane portion reads "When fifty years ago my brother Charles and I, in the simplicity of our hearts, told the good people of England that unless they *knew* their sins were forgiven, they were under the wrath and curse of God, I marvel, Melville, they did not stone us!" [emphasis his][22] (On a related topic see Outler's comments on pages 200-201 of volume 1 regarding Wesley attenuating his early tendency to drive his hearers to extremes of despair when "convicting" them of sin).

### Sin, the Believer and Perfection

The doctrine of Christian perfection was one that "God peculiarly entrusted to the Methodists" according to Wesley's *Journal* entry of February 6, 1789. It was also a doctrine that caused much confusion and misunderstanding about the affections since it was "perfect love" which Wesley was preaching. If perfection were required, many wondered, would the Christian then have to be feeling only one thing, namely love, at all times?

First of all, we need to understand Wesley's understanding of perfection. The best summary of it is found in sermon 76 "On Perfection":

> This is the sum of perfection: It is all comprised in that one word, Love. The first branch of it is the love of God: And as he that loves God loves his brother also, it is inseparably connected with the second: 'Thou shalt love thy neighbor as thyself:' Thou shalt love every man as thy own soul, as Christ loved us. 'On these two commandments hang all the Law and the Prophets:' these contain the whole of Christian perfection. (#76, 74)

Later in this same sermon he says that another way to talk about this whole reality of perfection is in terms of acquiring the mind of Christ which includes "the whole disposition of his mind, all his affections, all his tempers, both toward God and man. Now, it is certain that as there was no evil affection in him, so no good affection was wanting." (#76, 74)

Yet it was clear, to Wesley above all, that Christians did in fact sin. Indeed, sermon 13 "On Sin in Believers" was concerned solely with "inward sin: any sinful temper, passion, or affection...any disposition contrary to the mind which was in Christ." (#13, 320) It is this kind of sin which can *remain* even though Christ *reigns* (#13, 323), or, as he says later in this sermon, Christians have crucified the flesh with its affections and lusts [Galatians 5:24] yet this flesh remains "and often struggles to break free from the cross." (#13, 329) As Outler points out in his introduction to both "On Sin in Believers" and "The Repentance of Believers," Wesley wrote these sermons in the 1760s but inserted them in the first volume of his *Sermons* after some decidedly un-Wesleyan formulations of the doctrine of perfection were starting to circulate, especially among the Moravians. "Sinless perfection" was not Wesley's term of choice, though some of his writing had been interpreted in that direction. See Outler's note on Sermon 40 "Christian Perfection" where he points out how Wesley sometimes spoke unguardedly about "perfection." (107)

What we have, then, is an affectional *telos* for the Christian life - perfect love - which is in no way contradicted or vitiated by affectional sin even in the justifed believer. This reflects a basic feature of Wesley's theology: that justification and sanctification are two closely related yet logically separable realities. "A man may be in God's favour though he *feel* sin; but not if he *yields* to it." [emphasis his] (#13, 332) We still need the "Repentance of Believers" (sermon 14) because while we are born again at the moment of justification, we are not entirely changed, nor wholly transformed, "Far from it." (#14, 351) Acknowledging the reality of sin, however, should not keep us from having an "uneasiness for the want of [entire sanctification]," we need to "hunger and thirst after it." (#14, 351)

Having perfect love as our goal, then, does not mean that we must always have some constancy of inner *feeling*, which any psychologist (or any sentient being, for that matter) would say is impossible. Wesley never maintains that total control over the inner realm is somehow the norm for Christianity. In fact, inner feelings are not the issue at stake here. Just as we saw in the *Notes*, *feelings* can come and go, but it is the more enduring aspects of the affectional make-up which speak to the question of whether or not someone is a Christian:

> A man may have *pride* in him, may think of himself in *some particulars* above what he ought to think (and so be *proud* in that particular) and yet not be a proud man in his *general* character....Resentment of an affront is sin. It is anomia, disconformity to the law of love. This has existed in me a thousand times. Yet it did not, and does not, *reign*....Here, therefore, as in ten thousand instances, there is *sin* without either *guilt* or *power*. [emphasis his] (#13, 330-331)

(For other discussions of how negative affections can exist in the justified, though not yet sanctified, believer, see sermons 41 "Wandering Thoughts," 46 "The Wilderness State," 47 "Heaviness Through Manifold Temptations." See also Outler's notes in Volume 1 about how Wesley repudiated "sinless perfection," pages 328, 333, 346.)

### Works and the Heart

John Wesley was active in the world. He was not given to long solitary retreats or extended periods of withdrawn meditation. The sermons show us (as we have already seen in the *Notes*) that his very emphasis on the religious affections as the "marks of the new birth" is precisely what led him into the world of action and society, not something that tempted him away from it. The conceptual linkage between a right heart and right works, in fact, moves in both directions: right works require a right heart and a right heart requires right works.

That "right works require a right heart" is seen throughout the sermons. Even in the first sermon of the corpus, "Salvation by Faith," we read that "Only corrupt fruit grows on a corrupt tree." (#1, 118) Discourse six on the Sermon on the Mount (number 26) is concerned to show "how all our actions likewise, even those that are indifferent in their own nature, may be made holy and good and acceptable to God, by a pure and holy intention. Whatever is done without this, he largely declares, is of no value before God." (#26, 573) Again in "On Perfection" we see that "Holiness of life" arises from "holiness of heart." (#76, 75) This is stated most starkly, perhaps, in number 7 "The Way to the Kingdom":

> Yea, two persons may do the same outward work-- suppose, feeding the hungry, or clothing the naked-- and in the meantime one of these may be truly religious and the other have no religion at all; for the one may act from the love of God, and the other from the love of praise. So manifest is it that although true religion naturally leads to every good word and work, yet the real nature thereof lies deeper still, even in 'the hidden man of the heart.' (#7, 220)[23]

Similarly, that a right heart requires right works is equally plain in the sermons. The most extended attention to this topic is sermon 24 the fourth discourse on the Sermon on the Mount. Here he begins by saying "The beauty of holiness, of that inward man of the heart which is renewed after the image of God, cannot but strike every eye

which God hath opened, every enlightened understanding."
(#24, 531) Shortly after this he states:

> If religion therefore were carried no farther than this
> they could have no doubt concerning it--they should
> have no objection against pursuing it with the whole
> ardour of their souls. But why, say they, is it clogged
> with other things? What need of loading it with *doing*
> and *suffering*? These are what damps the vigor of the
> soul and sinks it down to earth again. Is it not enough
> to 'follow after charity'? To soar upon the wings of
> love? Will it not suffice to worship God, who is a
> Spirit, with the spirit of our minds, without
> encumbering ourselves with outward things, or even
> thinking of them at all? (#24, 531-532, emphasis his.)

The answer to this is, of course, that "Christianity is
essentially a social religion, and that to turn it into a solitary
one is to destroy it; secondly, that to conceal this religion is
impossible, as well as utterly contrary to the design of its
author." (#24, 533) Explaining this he says "Ye may not flee
from men, and while ye are among them it is impossible to
hide your lowliness and meekness and those dispositions
whereby ye aspire to be perfect, as your Father in heaven is
perfect. Love cannot be hid any more than light; and least
of all when it shines forth in action..." (#24, 539) While it is
true that the "root of religion lies in the heart," it is also true
that such a root "cannot but put forth branches." (#24, 541)
    One of the clearest examples of a failure to act which
damages the affections is in not giving all one can. In
sermon 87 "The Danger of Riches" he sets forth his famous
dictum "Gain all you can, save all you can, give all you can"
and he also states there that riches allow us to gratify foolish
desires which lead to "unholy desires, and every unholy
passion and temper. We easily pass from these to pride,
anger, bitterness, envy, malice, revengefulness; to an

headstrong, unadvisable spirit--indeed, to every temper that is earthly, sensual, or devilish." (#87, 236) This same theme is seen in 108 "On Riches" as well as 122 "Causes of the Inefficacy of Christianity." In this last, he shows his increasing unhappiness over how his Methodists are handling their growing prosperity:

> ...you may find many that observe the First rule, namely, 'Gain all you can.' You may find a few that observe the Second, 'Save all you can:' But how many have you found that observe the Third rule, 'Give all you can?' Have you reason to believe that five hundred of these are to be found among fifty thousand Methodists? And yet nothing can be more plain, than that all who observe the two first rules without the third, will be twofold more the children of hell than ever were before. (#122, 91)[24]

### The Affections in the Sermons: Conclusions

Wesley's theological discourse, especially as found in the sermons, is so laden with affection-terms that it is possible to describe the entire pattern of salvation in terms of the process of gaining and deepening the pattern of affections which manifest the saving presence of God in human being. Prevenient grace draws us to attend to the things of God. Thus fixed on His self-giving love and our unworthiness, we feel *sorrow* for our sins and *fear* of judgment which lead to *repentance*. Seeing that we are justified by grace through faith brings forth *trust* in Christ, and we become filled with *love, joy, peace* and therefore *happiness*, while *anger* and *hatred* wither. These affections (which are the assurance of faith) become well-springs of action, disposing us to *love* our neighbor in concrete ways, and to attend to the means of grace which strengthen these affections. After a life of *love*, we become glorified into *pure love*, fully recovering the image of God lost through Adam and made reachable again through Christ.[25]

Wesley's picture of the Christian life, then, puts God (and his grace) first and last, but also allows for human intention, motive and action. The institutional church has an important role to play in the whole drama of salvation, but never as an end in itself and only as an instrument to bring about the ultimate reality of the Christian life: love of God and neighbor. To be perfect in love is to be fully sanctified.

With this sketch as background, let us now go on to consider some other works published by Wesley which will help us to understand the religious affections as he viewed them. We will focus especially on Wesley's abridgement of Jonathan Edwards' *Treatise on Religious Affections*. In many ways this work can be taken as a brief compendium of all of Wesley's views about the affections.

1. Abingdon *Works*, volume 1, 42, note 55.

2. *Ibid.*, 35, 52.

3. Curnock, editor, volume 6, 209.

4. *The Elusive Mr. Wesley* (Nashville: Abingdon Press, 1984) volume 1, 146.

5. *John Wesley and the Church of England* (Nashville: Abingdon Press, 1970) 110.

6. *Ibid.*

7. See Outler's "Introduction," 14 and Heitzenrater's *The Elusive Mr. Wesley*, 146.

8. Outler's "Introduction," 97.

9. Outler's "Introduction" to the Preface, 103.

10. *Ibid.*

11. *Ibid.*

12. *Ibid.*, 105.

13. *Ibid.*, 106.

14. *Ibid.*

15. *Ibid.*, 107.

16. Thanks to Drs. Albert Outler and Frank Baker, I was given access to the early sermons of John Wesley even before they were published in the Abingdon *Works* series. Though I used only the typescript "top copy" in my original research, for this book I have translated those references into the page references of the recently published Volume 4 of the *Sermons*. Similarly, I originally made use of the Jackson and Sugden editions for references to the other sermons. These works have now been superseded by the complete 4 volume edition of Abingdon Press. All references to Wesley's sermons will, accordingly, be from this now-standard edition. A complete listing of these sermons can be found in Appendix A of volume one of the *Works*, 705-6.

17. For the chronology of these sermons, see Appendix B of the Baker/Outler's *Sermons*, volume 1.

18. Cf. Augustine's *On Christian Doctrine* where he says that in heaven, faith will be replaced by vision, blessedness will replace hope and, of the earthly virtues, only love will survive and grow stronger. (Book I, number 38)

19. See, e.g., William Law's *A Serious Call to a Devout and Holy Life* and Jeremy Taylor's *Rules and Exercise of Holy Living and Holy Dying*.

20. For later sermons that pick-up this central theme of restoring the image of God and show how the affections are crucial for the task, see #59 "God's Love to Fallen Man," 423; #61 "The Mystery of Iniquity," 452; #62 "The End of Christ's Coming," 474-5, 482-3.

21. In light of this, I have to take exception to Outler's "Introductory Comment" to these three sermons. On page 267 he says "It was clear enough that Wesley's theory of religious knowledge was frankly intuitionist, but this had been all too easily misconstrued as a one-sided subjectivism." In order to rescue him from such "subjectivism" Outler interprets these three sermons as betraying the following logic:

> The main point to the discourses on 'The Witness of the Spirit' had been the *objective* ground of Christian assurance, *viz.*, the direct 'witness of the Spirit' as revealing to and convincing the believer of God's pardoning, regenerating, adoptive grace.

Here, in the sequel, [sermon 12] Wesley undertakes an analysis of the *subjective* side of this *experience* of grace. (#12, 299) [emphasis his]

My objection to this is his terming the witness of the Spirit as "objective." As God's grace is quite resistible on Wesley's terms, no witness will ever be "objective" in the sense of being independent or our evaluations of it. Therefore, I think it is more helpful to say that God is the *object* of the experience rather than saying that the direct witness is "objective." If Outler meant by his phraseology "not self-generated," and this is my suspicion, then we are in fundamental agreement, but I think my language is less susceptible to misinterpretation.

22. "An Investigation of the Definition of Justifying Faith..." (1809) 3, quoted in *Works*, volume 1, 154-5. Also see sermon number 55 "On the Trinity" (385) where Wesley says that the "experimental verity" of Marquis de Renty is for fathers in Christ, not babes. Also, on the same page, Wesley says that only one in twenty believers will "advert" to the "witness" but it is implied in what many of them say.

23. Also on this theme, see sermon nos. 27 (592); 30 (651); and 33 (698).

24. For more of Wesley's attacks on antinomianism see sermons 34-36 "The Original, Nature, Properties, and Use of the Law," and "The Law Established through Faith" Discourses I and II, as well as number 16 "The Means of Grace." Note sermon 92 "On Zeal" to see that Wesley places "zeal for works of mercy" only below "zeal for holy tempers" and *above* "zeal for works of piety" [e.g. receiving communion.]

25. For a summary of Wesley's thought almost as concise as this, and one which is filled with the language of the affections, see Sermon number 43 "The Scripture Way of Salvation."

# CHAPTER SIX

## True Religion and the Affections: Wesley's Other Publications and His Abridgement of Jonathan Edwards's *Treatise on Religious Affections*

"True Religion, in great part, consists in Holy Affections."

From the *Treatise on Religious Affections*.

### Wesley's Other Writings and Abridgements

Though it was his *Notes* on Scripture and his sermons which Wesley thought best summarized the theological essentials of the "Methodists," he also published thousands of pages of his *Journal*, wrote hundreds of letters, and published dozens of abridgements of various works, many of which express the distinctive elements of his theology. Accordingly, discussions of the religious affections are found throughout all of these different genres of literature. Let us here consider just a few selections.

### Wesley's Own Heart in the Journals and Letters

Wesley, sometimes called a "pious Pepys," recorded most of the important details of his life in journals and diaries and most of these he later published for the public to read. As *published* works, these were not just intended to be idiosyncratic musings but were seen as a way of carrying out his duty as a minister to proclaim the Gospel and exhort

127

his readers to a Christian life. Similarly, his letters, through which he carried out a kind of spiritual direction via the mail, were also intended to convey his views concerning the most important aspects of Christianity and thus are significant additional sources for his views.

There are two different kinds of material relating to the affections to be found in Wesley's journals and letters. One is made up of the many passages which lay-open Wesley's own spiritual life. The second is material which contain didactic statements about Christianity and the affections but which are often unrelated to Wesley's own struggles. Let us turn first to that material which portrays Wesley's own struggles with the affectional life.

The scope of this work provides no room for a full study of Wesley's character. Other researchers have begun to delve into this issue.[1] Here we will consider only a few selected passages relevant to Wesley's own spiritual life.

Wesley says in an early description of his growth in Christianity that at the age of 22, through reading Thomas à Kempis, he "began to see, that true religion was seated in the heart, and that God's law extended to all our thoughts as well as words and actions." (Curnock 1:466) But he soon came to think that Thomas was too strict, for Wesley saw no reason why humanity should be "perpetually miserable" or that "all mirth is vain and useless."[2] Even in 1725, then, we see the forming emphasis on happiness and joy as marks of the Christian life.

We see this again in his letter to "Aspasia" (Mary Pendarves) of July 19, 1731 which reads in part:

> ...I was made to be happy; to be happy I must love God; in proportion to my love of whom my happiness must increase. To love God I must be like him, holy as he is holy; which implies both the being pure from vicious and foolish passions and the being confirmed in those virtues and rational affections which God

comprises in the word "charity." In order to root those out of my soul and plant these in their stead I must use (1) such means as are ordered by God, (2) such as are recommended by experience and reason.[3]

But too one sided of an emphasis on the "inner" aspect of the affections also moved Wesley to comment, as in his journal entry of January 25, 1738 where he describes his acquaintance with the mystic writers

whose noble descriptions of union with God and internal religion made everything else appear mean, flat and insipid. But in truth, they made good works appear so too, yea, and faith itself, and what not? These gave me an entire new view of religion, nothing like anything I had had before. But alas! It was nothing like that religion which Christ and his apostles lived and taught. I had a plenary dispensation from all the commands of God....Thus were all the bands burst at once....Only, my present sense is this, All the other enemies of Christianity are triflers; the mystics are the most dangerous of all its enemies.[4]

In his journal of November 1, 1739 he also condemns the idea of "being still" (doing no works) (Curnock 2:312) and it is this issue which caused his ultimate break with the Moravians (see Curnock 2: 329-330).

Wesley's experiences during a meeting held in a room on Aldersgate street on May 24, 1738 are well known, but they nonetheless are worthy of a few comments here. Showing the transitivity or intentionality of emotion, Wesley states that before his Aldersgate experience he had faith "But still I had not this faith on its right object: I meant only faith in God, not faith in or through Christ." (Curnock, 1:471) But at that society meeting

About a quarter before nine, while he was describing the change which God works in the heart through faith in Christ, I felt my heart strangely warmed.  I felt I did trust in Christ, Christ alone for salvation; and an assurance was given me that He had taken away my sins, even mine, and saved me from the law of sin and death....But it was not long before the enemy suggested, 'This cannot be faith; for where is thy joy?' Then was I taught that peace and victory over sin are essential to faith in the Captain of our salvation; but that, as to the transports of joy that usually attend the beginning of it, especially in those who have mourned deeply, God sometimes giveth, sometimes withholdeth them, according to the counsels of His own will. (Curnock 1:475-6)

Both the proclamation of the felt presence of salvation, as well as the acknowledgement of its felt absence, then, were part of Wesley's experience and message from the beginning.  That there was never a pretense of an unbroken continuity of felt joy, or even peace or love or faith, in his own life can be seen in several despairing journal entries.  Seven months after his "conversion," (January 4, 1739) he stated that "I am not a Christian now."  Even more strongly 27 years later he claims in a letter to his brother Charles that "I do not love God.  I never did....Therefore I am only an honest heathen."[5]

Despite such passing phases of his spiritual life, however, he always claimed that the radical change of conversion (his own and that of others) was real and he often described it in terms of the affections.  "I have seen (as far as a thing of this kind can be seen) very many persons changed in a moment from the spirit of fear, horror, despair, to the spirit of love, joy, and peace, and from sinful desire, till then reigning over them, to a pure desire of doing the will of God."[6]  Thus, even though he knew there was no guarantee of constant feeling, he always asserted that to be a Christian meant having certain affectional capacities. Such an emphasis lead others to say he was "beside himself"[7] and to give naturalistic, debunking explanations of the dramatic conversions his ministry facilitated[8], but his linking of Christianity and the religious affections never changed during his entire life.

### Theological Views in the Journals and Letters

But Wesley did not fill his journals and letters with tales of his inner life. On the contrary, he was more a reporter of, and commentator upon, the doings of others than he was a self-centered spiritual physician constantly taking his own spiritual pulse. Let us examine just a few passages where he speaks normatively about the affections, the believer and the church.

In a letter to Richard Morgan, Sr. on January 15, 1734 Wesley claims that religion is not a saying of prayers or anything added to an otherwise worldly life but is instead "a constant ruling habit of soul; a renewal of our minds in the image of God; a recovery of the divine likeness..."[9] This same theme is seen in a letter of later that same year to Samuel Wesley, Sr. where Wesley defines holiness as "not fasting, or bodily austerity, or any other external means of improvement, but that inward temper to which all these are subservient, a renewal of soul in the image of God..."[10]

Speaking about what is most important for the Christian life to James Erskine, Lord Grange, in 1745 Wesley wrote "I am more assured that love is of God than that any opinion whatsoever is."[11] In 1749 he wrote a long letter to Conyers Middleton (part of which was later reprinted as *A Plain Account of Genuine Christianity*) and in this letter he states that Christianity "is holiness and happiness, the image of God impressed on a created spirit, a fountain of peace and love springing up into everlasting life."[12]  Writing to the *Westminster Journal* Wesley stated boldly "The whole ingredients of our religion are love, joy, peace, longsuffering, gentleness, goodness, fidelity, meekness, temperance."[13]

It is also clear from Wesley's letters and journals that this religion of the heart was *not* a religion of mere *feeling*. In his *Journal* Wesley criticizes a Mr. Simpson because "he is led into a thousand mistakes by one wrong principle (the same which many either ignorantly or wickedly ascribe to the body of the people called Methodists), the making inward impressions his rule of action, and not the written word."[14]  Again, in a letter to Thomas Olivers, Wesley states that "Barely to feel no sin, or to feel constant peace, joy, and love, will not prove the point."[15]  Wesley's mature position - that it is the *cause* (the object) of religious feelings and the *behaviors* that these feelings lead to which are crucial for his affection-related vision of Christianity - is seen in his response to *A Seasonable Antidote Against Popery* where he states that we must not reject all inward feelings, "but only those which are without faith or repentance. [The author of the tract says] 'If you have not these, to pretend to any other feelings is vain and delusive.' I say so too."[16]

In his letter to William Law of 1756 Wesley calls his old teacher to be faithful to his own stated position against mixing religion and philosophy, for "so far as you add philosophy to religion, just so far you spoil it."[17]  And this emphasis on the heart over against mere opinion or anything less concrete than lived experience can also be found in his letter to Samuel Walker of Truro of September 3, 1756. There Wesley says:

> I have one point in view - to promote, so far as I am able, vital, practical religion; and by the grace of God to beget, preserve, and increase the life of God in the soul of men. On this single principle I have hitherto

proceeded, and taken no step but in subserviency to it.[18]

So firmly did Wesley hold that embodying the Christian affections was the key point in being a Christian that in a letter to his sister Emilia he warned her that her lack of thankfulness to God and man rendered her as much a sinner as "whores and murderers."[19]  Placing the central emphasis on the disposition of the heart allowed Wesley to be tolerant with regard to most of those issues which many contentious Christians staked their whole identity on.  To Mrs. Howton in October of 1783 he wrote "It is the glory of the people called Methodists that they condemn none for their opinions or modes of worship.  They think and let think, and insist upon nothing but faith working by love."[20]

To make sure that this "faith working by love" did not degenerate into a works righteousness, Wesley said the following to "John Smith" in 1745:

"I would rather say faith is 'productive of all Christian *holiness*' than 'of all Christian *practice*'; because men are so exceeding apt to rest in 'practice', so called, I mean in *outside religion*; whereas *true religion* is eminently seated in the heart, renewed in the image of him that created us [emphasis his].[21]

Writing in the next year to the same "John Smith," Wesley shows clearly the priority of love in the hierarchy of the affections:

I would just add that I regard even faith itself not as an *end*, but a *means* only.  The end of the commandment is love--of every command, of the whole Christian dispensation.  Let this love be attained, by whatever means, and I am content; I desire no more.  All is well if we love the Lord our God with all our heart, and our neighbor as ourselves.

Even the role of the church is ultimately defined in relation to the affections for Wesley. Again to "John Smith" Wesley asks "'What is the end of all ecclesiastical order?' Is it not to bring souls from the power of Satan to God, and to build them up in his fear and love?  Order, then, is so far valuable as it answers these ends:  and if it answers them not, it is nothing worth."[22]

**Wesley's Other Publications**

The central place that the religious affections hold in Wesley's theology, and the particular grammar which he attributes to them, are displayed throughout Wesley's other writings.  For example, consider:

* In the opening section of *An Earnest Appeal to Men of Reason and Religion* Wesley shows that love is the beginning of Christian doctrine and also the primary way of conceiving of God.[23]  He also tersely describes the goal of his ministry by saying "You ask me what I would do with them.  I would make them virtuous and happy, easy in them-selves, and useful to others" (51).  He then goes on to emphasize that happiness is the proper concern of religion ("are you *now* happy?" 60ff) and that "inward" religion, the religion of the tempers, is what he preaches (63, 88ff).  In *A Farther Appeal*, Part I, he states that while we *are* meant to feel peace, joy and love, the best proof of being led by the Spirit is a "thorough change and renovation of mind and heart, and the leading a new and holy life" (140-141).

* In his *A Plain Account of Christian Perfection* he guards against a religion of feeling by admonishing his readers to try all things such as "dreams, voices, impressions, visions, or revelations" by the Scriptures in order to judge if they are from God.[24]

* In the Preface to his *Christian Library* he states again that the Christian religion is "nothing stranger, or harder to understand than this, 'We love Him, because He first loved us.'"[25]

* In his Preface to the book that most clearly links the aesthetic to the religious, his *Hymns and Sacred Poems*, he clearly warns against reducing religion into feeling states by pointing out that "The Gospel of Christ knows of no religion but social; no holiness but social holiness. 'Faith working by love' is the length and breadth and depth and height of Christian perfection."[26]

* That many of the prayers found in his *Collection of Forms of Prayer* are petitions for the gracious affections and deliverance from the evil affections.[27]

* That one of his main concerns about the character of the clergy, as seen in his *Address to the Clergy*, is that they be filled with the affections of God.[28]

* That question 74 of the so-called "Larger Minutes" puts "Methodism" and "heart-holiness" in apposition.[29]

* In his long "Answer to the Rev. Mr. Church" Wesley states directly how Christians *must* speak about the "inner" life *without* uncritically proclaiming a religion of feeling. There he asks:

Do you reject inward feelings *toto genere*?
Then you reject both the love of God and of
neighbor. For, if these cannot be inwardly
felt, nothing can. You reject all joy in the
Holy Ghost; for if we cannot be sensible of
this, it is no joy at all. You reject the peace
of God, which, if it be not felt in the inmost
soul, is a dream, a notion, an empty name.
You therefore reject the whole inward
kingdom of God; that is, in effect, the whole
gospel of Jesus Christ.[30]

All of this is to say nothing about the many hymns with
affection-related themes which the Wesley brothers
published.[31] Nor have we discussed the many abridgements
which Wesley published, and he abridged and published
hundreds of books and pamphlets during his lifetime. Many
of these abridgements which Wesley published were on
themes germane to the "inner" life.[32] One of these
abridgements, however, is worthy of special attention
because in many ways it can be seen as a compact summary
of many of Wesley's views about the religious affections.
This is his abridgement of Jonathan Edwards's *Treatise on
Religious Affections*.

### The *Treatise on Religious Affections*[33]

Jonathan Edwards was born in East Windsor,
Connecticut in the year of John Wesley's birth, 1703 (d.
1758). Educated at Yale, he had a lifelong fascination with
both philosophy and natural science as well as theology.
Locke and Newton were his intellectual companions every
bit as much as Calvin was. Such interests were reflected in
his writings as well as his readings, as seen in his papers
titled "Of Insects," "The Mind" and even "Of Being."[34]

While his *Freedom of the Will*[35] is usually taken to be his major contribution to theology, Edwards is more widely known for his sermon "Sinners in the Hands of an Angry God" which is most notable for its vivid depiction of the end that awaits the reprobate. Unfortunately, neither *Freedom of the Will* nor his sermon give a true picture of the broad scope and creative nature of his work. Edwards was much more concerned with beauty and love than he was with either humanity's bondage to sin or the nature of hell.[36] It is these wider interests that are most relevant for our concerns.

Roland Delattre in his *Beauty and Sensibility in the Thought of Jonathan Edwards* claims that Edwards understood Divine Being to be most immediately and powerfully present to humanity as beauty.[37] This beauty is known through our sensibility; i.e., it is *felt*, and not merely intellectually inferred by the understanding. Saving knowledge of God, then, is available only in and through the enjoyment of God. The fullness of God is encountered as a living reality "only according to the degree to which men find in [God] their entire joy and happiness, the fulfillment of their aesthetic-affectional being."[38]

This emphasis on the sensible apprehension of God, when linked with Edwards's appreciation for the philosophy of John Locke, has been taken by some of Edwards's interpreters as showing that Edwards's epistemology was nothing more than philosophical empiricism.[39] But Terrence Erdt has recently shown that a "sense of the heart" or a "sweetness" (*suavitas*) can be found in Calvin's thought, so that Edwards's emphasis on feeling and the "heart" has a rootage in the *theological* tradition which is deeper than is often suspected.[40] But regardless of its historical roots, Edwards's affectional "sense of the heart" was at the center of his psychology, epistemology, ethics and, indeed, his whole theology.

## Wesley and Edwards

It was Edwards's theoretical concern with the nature of religious experience and, more importantly, his burning practical desire to have such experience widely propagated, that put Edwards and Wesley on common ground. Wesley's first contact with Edwards's writings came in 1738. Wesley was traveling from London to Oxford when he "read the truly surprising narrative of the conversions lately wrought in and about the town of Northampton, in New England. Surely 'this is the Lord's doing and it is marvelous in our eyes.'"[41]

What he read was Edwards's *A Faithful Narrative of the Surprising Work of God...*[42] which was to be the first of five works of Edwards that Wesley would abridge and publish.[43] The other four works which Wesley published also had direct bearing on the subjects of Christian experience and evangelism. These were *The Distinguishing Marks of a Work of the Spirit of God* (written in 1741, Wesley's abridgement published in 1744); *Some Thoughts Concerning the Present Revival of Religion in New England* (1742, 1745); *The Life of David Brainerd*, who was Edwards's son-in-law and a missionary to the Indians (1749, 1768); and, of course, the *Treatise on Religious Affections* (1746, 1773).

These five works by Edwards represent the largest number of separate works by one author that Wesley was to abridge and publish under his own name.[44] The influence of Edwards on Wesley was so strong that Albert C. Outler has said that Edwards was a "major source" of Wesley's theology, and that, indeed, Wesley's encounter with Edwards's early writings was one of four basic factors that set the frame for Wesley's thought.[45]

This is not to say, though, that there were no important differences between the two, for there were. Wesley was familiar with Edwards's *Freedom of the Will* but he published no abridgement of it and, instead, attacked the views contained in it in his "Thoughts Upon Necessity."[46] Wesley thought that Edwards's denial of human freedom made nonsense of the moral life. In general, anything that smacked of Calvinistic "irresistible grace" or "unconditional election" Wesley was careful to excise from his abridgements of Edwards's work.

Edwards also had his disagreements with Wesley. In fact, the only record of Edwards referring to Wesley was a disparaging remark which he made about Wesley's views on perfection.[47] If one were to give an irenic reading of their differences, one might say that while Wesley and Edwards agreed about the sovereignty of God, Edwards expressed this sovereignty through his Calvinist doctrines of predestination and the bondage of the will, and Wesley expressed the same thing by emphasizing prevenient grace and the perfecting possibilities of the Spirit. Both the continuities and the differences between these two men can be seen in microcosm in Wesley's abridgement of Edwards's most widely read book[48], his *Treatise on Religious Affections*.

### Wesley's Abridgement of Edwards's *Treatise*

The task of discerning a man's views by looking at how he abridged another man's work must be approached with caution. Frank Baker in his article "A Study of John Wesley's Readings" states that one of the ways that Wesley dealt with a "dangerous" book was by publishing an expurgated version of it.[49] This might lead one to believe that Wesley's version of the *Treatise on Religious Affections* was merely the lesser of two evils: since the book was already in print, Wesley may have thought that it would be better if his followers read his version rather than Edwards's (if they had to read it at all). If this were the case, the abridgement would be less an endorsement of Edwards's views and more a hostile toleration of them.

Such doubts about attributing the views stated in the abridgement to the abridger are reinforced when it is noted that books did in fact appear in the first edition of Wesley's *Christian Library*[50] which contained views contradicting Wesley's own.[51] But this is less of a problem than it first appears to be, for the publication of the offending passages was more the result of Wesley's hasty abridging than any inconsistency in Wesley's thought. Wesley later corrected the *Christian Library* to remove the contradictions and the expurgated version was published after his death by Thomas Jackson in 1827.

There is one compelling piece of evidence, though, that allows us to take Wesley's abridgement of Edwards's *Treatise* as representative of Wesley's own views, namely, that Wesley specifically endorsed the book. Wesley did not always write a preface for the books that he published, but in the case of the *Treatise* he did. In this preface, he both distances himself from some parts of the original *Treatise* and recommends the portion he retained. The end of this preface reads "Out of this dangerous heap, wherein much wholesome food is mixed with much deadly poison, I have selected many remarks and admonitions which may be of great use to the children of God. May God write them in the hearts of all that desire to walk as Christ also walked!"[52] My purpose now is to spell-out what Wesley considered poison and what he considered food.

**What Wesley Deleted**

Determining what Wesley left out of the *Treatise* is more difficult than one might first suspect, since it appears that Wesley did not work from the original edition. John E. Smith has determined that Wesley worked from an abridgement made by William Gordon, published in London in 1762.[53] Gordon, who is listed as an "independent minister" in the *Dictionary of National*

*Biography*[54], reduced the text by more than one third, omitted many notes and rewrote the text in hundreds of places. This means that in order to be sure that any omission was truly Wesley's omission, all three texts - Edwards's, Gordon's and Wesley's - must be compared.

But determining exactly what Wesley left out would be crucially important only if our purpose were to chronicle the differences between Edwards and Wesley on the topic of religious affections. Our main concern, however, is to see what Wesley appreciated and approved of in the *Treatise*, not what he disliked. So, instead of a lengthy three-way textual comparison, I will just make a few general remarks about Gordon's abridgement and Wesley's deletions before moving on to consider what Wesley liked about the book.

First of all, while he did remove much of the original text, Gordon's appreciation of Edwards was much less critical than Wesley's. The original *Treatise* consisted of a preface and three major parts: Part I concerning the nature of the affections, Part II containing 12 signs that *cannot* be used to judge whether or not particular affections are gracious, and Part III which contains 12 distinguishing signs of "Truly Gracious and Holy Affections." Gordon retains all four basic parts of the work, and in Parts II and III both sets of 12 signs are fully represented. His excisions and revisions, which apparently occurred most often when he determined that Edwards was "too refined for common capacities"[55], do not, in my judgment, pervert the essential thrust of Edwards's work.

Wesley was a much more ruthless editor. Whereas Gordon's abridgement was about two-thirds of the original, Wesley's was one-sixth. He cut not only Edwards's preface, but the second, third and fourth of the twelve signs of Part III in their entirety, as well as considerably reducing the explanations of the remaining signs. One sign (the seventh) was so reduced that Wesley did not even bother to number it and, instead, merely included a brief summary of it in the

preceding section.[56]  The omissions that Wesley made
usually fall into one of two categories, both of which are
alluded to in Wesley's Preface.  These two categories of
edited material might be defined as 1) Calvinistic and 2)
overly "subtle."

As he made clear in his Preface, Wesley thought that
Edwards's purpose in writing the *Treatise* was to show that
backsliders were never true believers in the first place.  In
other words, Wesley saw the *Treatise* as a Calvinistic tract on
the perseverance of the saints.  Wesley claimed that
Edwards's attempt to defend such an indefensible doctrine
led him to heap together "so many curious, subtle,
metaphysical distinctions, as are sufficient to puzzle the
brain, and confound the intellects, of all the plain men and
women of the universe; and to make them doubt of, if not
wholly deny, all the work which God had wrought in their
souls."[57]  After this broadside, Wesley goes on to admit, as
quoted above, that there is much wholesome food mixed in
with the "deadly poison."

As others have pointed out, it seems clear that Wesley
misunderstood Edwards's purpose in writing the *Treatise*.[58]
Edwards was trying to show valid signs for distinguishing
true from false piety or "religion," not explain away the fact
of backsliding.  Wesley might justifiably be accused of being
somewhat defensive here - seeing Edwards's Calvinism
operating where it really was not.  True, Edwards does
mention the "elect" in a few places, and other Calvinistic
tendencies which Wesley altered can surely be seen in the
original, but Wesley's Preface mischaracterizes the tenor of
the *Treatise* as polemical when it is in fact constructive.
Since Wesley was caught-up in heated debate with the
Calvinists at the time of the abridgement, his defensiveness
can at least be understood, if not justified.[59]

The most substantive passages that Wesley omitted
from the *Treatise*, however, are not the overtly Calvinistic
ones, but the overly "subtle" ones which Wesley said "puzzle"

and "confound" plain-thinking humanity. Wesley shared Edwards's interest in science and philosophy, but edification was Wesley's ultimate criterion when evaluating the written word. Edwards was a brilliant speculative thinker who incorporated many of his philosophical theories into his theological works. Because of this, Wesley encountered much that could be dispensed with. This can be seen especially in two of the three signs that Wesley omitted.

The second of Edwards's twelve signs states that the "first objective ground of gracious affections is the transcendently excellent and amiable nature of divine things"[60]; the third sign says that holy affections are founded on the "loveliness of the moral excellency of divine things."[61] In these two signs, we can see the metaphysics of "beauty" and "excellence" which Delattre has declared to be the lynch-pin of Edwards's speculations.[62] Wesley was probably content with Edwards's point (made in many other places) that divine things are the object of gracious affections, and that extended discussions of the "loveliness" or "moral excellency" of these divine things were therefore dispensable.

Conjecture about why Wesley deleted the fourth sign is more difficult, for it asserts something which Wesley would not want to deny - the intellectual component in the affections ("Gracious affections do arise from the mind's being enlightened, rightly and spiritually to understand of apprehend divine things."[63]) Certainly Wesley was never tempted, as Luther was, to "tear-out the eyes of reason" in order to promote faith. One can only guess that Wesley considered this sign to go too far in the other direction, i.e., that it could be taken as a kind of rationalism. In this condensed volume, Wesley may have thought that there was not enough space for a sign that might give some support to those who advocated a mere "head" religion which bypassed the heart.

## What Wesley Retained

At the beginning of Part I, Edwards quotes the text of 1 Peter 1:8: "Whom having not seen ye love: In whom, though now you see him not, yet believing, ye rejoice with joy unspeakable and full of glory." In this text, Edwards sees the two archetypal exercises of true religion: Love to Christ and Joy in Christ. Based on this, he then formulates the proposition that he will defend throughout the entire book, that "True religion, in great part, consists in Holy Affections."[64] His first step in this process is to define what affections are.

According to Edwards, the "affections of the mind" are "the more vigorous and sensible exercises of the will." (311) In drawing this out, Edwards goes on to say that God has imbued the soul with two faculties: the understanding which is capable of perception and speculation, and the inclination or will which either is pleased or displeased, approving or rejecting the things perceived. The mind with regard to the exercises of the will is called the heart. The crucial point here is that the affections are not exercised apart from the understanding.

Edwards makes his anthropology even more explicit when he says that it is the mind and not the body that is the proper seat of the affections. Herein lies the difference between affections and passions as well. Passions are more sudden, have a more violent effect on the "animal spirits," and in them "the mind is less in its own command." (312)

The next section of Part I consists of several points which attempt to show that a great part of true religion lies in the affections. These range from the more speculative arguments ("The religion of heaven consists much in affection") (316), to arguments based on observations of human behavior ("affections are the springs of men's actions") (313) to arguments based strictly on Scripture ("Holy Scripture places religion in the affections," and "The

Scriptures place the sin of the heart much in hardness of heart.") (313, 316)  From these and other arguments, Edwards draws these inferences:

1) That we cannot discard all religious affections. (317)

2) That "such means are to be desired, as have a tendency to move the affections." (318)

3) That "if true religion lies much in the affections, what cause have we to be ashamed, that we are no more affected with the great things of religion!" (318)  In other words, we are to be held morally and spiritually accountable for having certain affectional capacities.

This leads to Part II.

Having established the connections between true religion and the affections in Part I, Edwards now moves on to the theme that occupies the largest part of the book: distinguishing the holy and gracious affections from those that are not.  Part II is a discussion of 12 features of so-called "religious affections."  Edwards asserts that these 12 "signs" can*not* give certain knowledge as to whether or not affections are "truly gracious."

One can imagine the sobering effect that these negative points must have had on many of the "spirit-filled Christians" of Edwards (and Wesley's) day.  Among the most interesting of the "signs" which are *not* necessarily indicative of grace are points number 1 (that religious affections are raised very high, 320); 2 (that they have great effects on the body, 321); 4 (that the persons did not make the affections themselves, 324-325); and 5 (that they come with texts of Scripture. 327)  Point number 3 can serve as a warning to all garrulous theologians of any age (that it is no sign to be fluent, fervent and abundant in talking of the things of religion. 324)

The final four signs, when seen together, show that, for Edwards, we can never know how another person's soul is seen by the eyes of God by observing their outward behavior. People can: spend much time in religion and worship (333); praise God with their mouths (334); be confident that their experience is divine (335); or convince other people of their godliness (342) without being assured that their affections are gracious. This makes an important point about the entire *Treatise*. It is to be an aid for one's own spiritual quest, not a guidebook for the judgment of others.

Part III of the *Treatise* is perhaps the most important section, for this is where Edwards explains what *are* valid signs of gracious and holy affections. The first sign is that gracious affections arise from "spiritual, divine and supernatural" influences on the heart. (343) The Spirit of God gives the believer a new "spiritual sense" (346) through which one has access to the divine things.

The second sign in Wesley's abridgement (Edwards's fifth sign) states that gracious affections are accompanied by a conviction of the reality and certainty of divine things. This conviction is not some sort of vague mysticism, or a certainty about the existence of "divine things" in general as we see, for instance, in the thought of Schleiermacher. It is instead a "conviction of the truth of the great things of the Gospel." (346) The title of the *Treatise* may sound as if the book is about generic religious experience, but, in reality, the positivity of the Christian religion is constantly and unashamedly asserted. We can also see here the intellectual nature, and object-relatedness, of the affections for Edwards and Wesley.

The sixth sign states that gracious affections are attended with "evangelical humiliation," i.e., a conviction of one's own "utter insufficiency, despicableness and odiousness, with an answerable frame of heart, arising from a discovery of God's holiness." (349)[65]   On this point, it is flatly put that "They that are destitute of this, have not true religion, whatever profession they may make." (349)   For Edwards (as for Wesley), humility is pervasive, it is a quality of all the other affections, and therein lies an important safeguard against "enthusiasm."

The material contained in the seventh sign in the original is treated in just a few unnumbered paragraphs by Wesley.  This is perhaps because this sign simply states that gracious affections are attended with a change in the nature of the affected person, which is really already implied in several of the other signs (e.g. numbers 6, 8, 9, 11, 12 in the original).

The eighth and ninth signs show that while false affections have a tendency to harden the heart, truly gracious affections promote the spirit that appeared in Christ (#8), a tenderness of spirit (#9). In these sections, Edwards lays special emphasis on love, meekness, quietness, forgiveness and mercy. From the very beginning, of course, Edwards has said that love is the first and chief of the affections - the "fountain" of all gracious affections (316) - but it is not until this eighth sign that we are given an overall view of what specific additional affections are, in fact, "religious."

The tenth sign is that gracious affections have beautiful symmetry and proportion.  While there are echoes here of Edwards's philosophical contention that we know God through beauty, there is also something more important being stressed.  In saying, for example, that love of God must be yoked with love of man, or that having hope does not mean jettisoning holy fear, Edwards is laying out his own "grammar" of the affections, his view of how these affections form and determine the shape of the human life and how they interact with each other.  The elucidation of

this "grammar" is the main theological task of the entire
*Treatise*.

The eleventh sign states that gracious affections
increase the longing for spiritual attainments while the false
affections tend to make one rest satisfied. This can be seen
as a corrective against those who might think that Edwards
is about cultivating religious experiences for their own sake.
This theme reaches its culmination in the twelfth and final
sign where the emphasis is shifted completely away from
inner experience to the necessary fruits of the affections:
works of love.

This last sign (the explanation of which is by far the
longest of the twelve in both the original and in Wesley's
abridgement) contains many arguments for Christian
practice as the chief of all the evidences of a "saving
sincerity" in religion. So much is practice emphasized here
that Edwards feels compelled to answer two objections that
might arise regarding the importance of the works:  the
objection that Christian experience is to be the central sign
of grace, and that emphasizing works could lead to a works-
righteousnes. Edwards smoothly answers these objections
by showing that "experience" and "practice" cannot be
separated, and that making a "righteousness" of experience
is just as heretical as a works righteousness. (372-376)

### Conclusions

We can see in the *Treatise*, then, all of the major points
of Wesley's heart-centered theology:  the close relations
between reason and emotion; the constant checks against
self-deception; the transitive or object-ive nature of the
affections; the central importance of the love of, and joy in,
God; and, finally, the dispositional nature of the emotions -
the fact that the truly Christian affections compel the
believer to live constructively in the social world.

The evidence already displayed is over-whelming in presenting a picture of what Wesley meant when he said that true religion consists, in great part, of religious affections. A picture of Wesley's theology has emerged which counters many of the common caricatures of him as espousing an unreflective piety, or making uncritical uses of appeals to experience. This now being thoroughly established, let us see how Wesley's heart-centered theology might be integrated into the contemporary theological scene.

1. See *John Wesley and Authority: A Psychological Perspective* by Robert L. Moore (Missoula: Scholar's Press, 1979); *John Wesley and the Bible: A Psychological Perspective* by Thorvald Källstad (Stockholm: NYA Bokförlags Aktiebolaget, 1974); and *John Wesley* by Stanley Ayling (Nashville: Abingdon, 1979).

2. Baker, ed., *Letters* volume 1, 162-163.

3. Quoted in Heitzenrater, Richard P., *The Elusive Mr. Wesley* (Nashville: Abingdon, 1984) volume 1, 57.

4. Quoted in Heitzenrater, 95-96.

5. *Letters*, Telford, ed., volume 5, 16.

6. See his *Journal* for May, 1739, quoted in Heitzenrater, 110.

7. Curnock, volume 2, 193.

8. Heitzenrater, 110, quoting the *Journal* for May of 1739.

9. Quoted in Heitzenrater, 70f.

10. Heitzenrater, 72, quoting the letter of 12/10/1734.

11. Baker, ed., *Letters* volume 2, 128.

12. Telford, ed., volume 2, 383.

13. *Letters*, volume 4, 131.

14. *Journal*, Curnock, ed., volume 3, 26.

15. *Letters*, volume 3, 212.

16. *Letters*, volume 3, 249-50. This passage, as well as those found in the two quotes immediately preceding it, were quoted in Mark Horst's Ph.D. dissertation "Christian Understanding and the Life of Faith in John Wesley's Thought" (Yale University, 1985). Since his dissertation first appeared in the same year that mine did, I

was unacquainted with his research until I had the opportunity to revise my dissertation for publication. I happily find his work to be reinforcing to my basic thesis about the importance of the affections for Wesley's theology. The reader is invited to consider Horst's views in both his dissertation and his article "Wholeness and Method in Wesley's Theology" in *Quarterly Review* (volume 7, no. 2, Summer 1987), 11-23.

17. *Ibid.*, volume 3, 332.

18. Quoted in Baker's *John Wesley and the Church of England* (Nashville: Abingdon, 1970) 118.

19. Baker, ed., *Letters* volume 2, 100.

20. Telford, ed., *Letters* volume 7, 190. See also his sermon "The Way to the Kingdom" and "The Character of a Methodist," section 1.

21. Baker, ed., *Letters* volume 2, 179, letter of 12/30/1745.

22. *Ibid.*, 206. Cf. Curnock volume 6, 167-8 where Wesley says that it would take only 100 preachers who "fear nothing but sin and desire nothing but God" to set up the kingdom of heaven on earth.

23. Oxford *Works*, volume 11, 45-51.

24. Jackson *Works*, volume 11, 429.

25. *Ibid.*, volume 14, 222.

26. *Ibid.*, volume 14, 321. See also Appendix I "Thoughts on the Power of Music" where Wesley asserts that things like counterpoint and harmony do not add to the goal of building up the affections and hence should be avoided. (766-9) Regardless of the truth of such pronouncements, his single-mindedness regarding the affections is nonetheless apparent.

27. *Ibid.*, volume 11, 203ff, especially 204, 208, etc.

28. *Ibid.*, volume 10, 486-7.

29. *Ibid.*, volume 8, 336.

30. *Ibid.*, 408.

31. See *A Collection of Hymns for the Use of the People Called Methodists*, Oxford *Works*, volume 7, and John Tyson's *Charles Wesley: A Reader* (forthcoming from Oxford University Press).

32. Including many of works by the early church fathers, as well as many more recent writers such as Scougal (*The Life of God in the Soul of Man*) and Francke (*Nicodemus: or A Treatise on the Fear of Man*), see Jackson *Works*, volume 14, 199-318.

33. Much of what follows originally appeared in a paper

presented to the Bicentennial Consultation of the United Methodist Church held at Emory University in 1983. This paper has been published in a collection of papers presented at this conference called *Wesleyan Theology Today* (Nashville: Abingdon Press). This paper also appeared in *Wesleyan Theological Journal* (Volume 19, Number 2, Fall 1984, 77-89).

34. Cf. *Scientific and Philosophical Writings*, volume 6 of his *Works* (New Haven: Yale University Press, 1980).

35. *Works*, volume 1 (New Haven: Yale University Press, 1957).

36. Actually, there are less than a dozen imprecatory sermons written by Edwards to be found among the more than a thousand which survive in manuscript form. See Sydney E. Ahlstrom, *A Religious History of the American People* (Garden City: Image Books, 1975) 370.

37. (New Haven: Yale University Press, 1968) 50. Delattre's analysis is based on all of Edwards's works, but he draws most heavily on the *Treatise on Religious Affections, The Nature of True Virtue* (Ann Arbor: University of Michigan Press, 1960) and the *Miscellanies* (forthcoming in the Yale *Works* series.)

38. *Ibid.*, 49.

39. The most influential exponent of this view was Perry Miller, especially in his *Jonathan Edwards* (New York: Wm. Stoane Associates, 1949).

40. See his *Jonathan Edwards: Art and the Sense of the Heart* (Amherst: University of Massachusetts Press, 1980) especially Chapter 1 "The Calvinist Psychology of the Heart."

41. Curnock, volume 2, 83-84.

42. The full title continues *in the Conversion of Many Hundred Souls in Northampton and the Neighboring Towns and Villages of New Hampshire in New England*, first written in 1736, Wesley's abridgement published in 1744.

43. For more detailed commentary on the abridgements, as well as an enlightening comparison of Wesley and Edwards, see Charles Rogers's "John Wesley and Jonathan Edwards" in *The Duke Divinity School Review* (volume 31, number 1, Winter, 1966, 20-38).

44. See Frank Baker's article "The Beginnings of American Methodism" *Methodist History* volume 2, number 1, October 1963, 9.

45. *John Wesley* (New York: Oxford University Press, 1964) 16. The other three factors, according to Outler, were his Aldersgate

conversion, his disenchantment with Moravianism and his vital reappropriation of his Anglican heritage.

46. Jackson *Works*, volume 10, 457-474.

47. *The Works of President Edwards*, volume 4, 118, quoted in Rogers, "John Wesley and Jonathan Edwards," 36.

48. Smith's "Introduction" to the *Treatise on Religious Affections*, 78. This work was first published in Boston in 1746, all quotes will be from volume 2 of the Yale University Press edition of his *Works*, John E. Smith, editor, Perry Miller, general editor (New Haven, 1959). Hereafter *RA*.

49. In *London Quarterly and Holborn Review*, 1943, 240.

50. See Frank Baker's *A Union Catalog of the Publications of John and Charles Wesley* (entry number 131) (Durham: Duke University Press, 1966) for the publication history of the *Christian Library*.

51. See T.W. Herbert's *John Wesley as Editor and Author* (Princeton: Princeton University Press, 1940) 26-27.

52. Wesley's abridgement, 308. Wesley's abridgement first appeared in his collected *Works* (volume 23, 177-279) 1773, reprinted in 1801, and later appeared in the second edition of his *Christian Library* (volume 30, 307-376) 1827. See Baker's *Union Catalog* (cited above) entry number 294 for the complete publication history. All references in this paper are to the *Christian Library* edition. Hereafter, *RA* (W).

53. *RA*, 79. Smith says that the chances of Wesley and Gordon independently making so many of the same omissions and substitutions is very small. Dr. Frank Baker's opinion, stated to me in a personal correspondence, concurs with Smith's.

54. Ed. by Leslie Stephen and Sidney Lee (New York: Macmillan and Co., 1890) volume 22, 235.

55. Gordon's abridgement, 78.

56. This omission of the number, though, might be the fault of Wesley's notoriously bad printers. Later in the text, the numbering jumps from IV to VI with V never appearing.

57. *RA*(W), 308.

58. See Smith's Introduction in *RA*, 80, and Rogers' "John Wesley and Jonathan Edwards," 30.

59. See John Allen Knight's "Aspects of Wesley's Theology After 1770" in *Methodist History*, volume 6 number 3, April, 1968, 33-

42.

60. *RA*, 240.

61. *Ibid.*, 253.

62. See *Beauty and Sensibility in the Thought of Jonathan Edwards*, (cited above) for in-depth discussions of primary and secondary beauty, the equivalence of beauty and excellence, and beauty as the "cordial consent of being to being-in-general."

63. *RA*, 266.

64. *RA* (W), 310. The following references will be made in the text and will refer to Wesley's abridgement.

65. To avoid confusion, I will refer to the signs by Edwards' enumeration.

# CHAPTER SEVEN

## Wesley's Practical Theology Reconsidered for the Post-Modern World

What is real, genuine Christianity?...a principle in the soul [and] a scheme of doctrine.

Christianity, taken in the latter sense, is that system of doctrine which describes the [Christian] character,...which promises it shall be mine (provided I will not rest till I attain), and which tells me how I may attain it.

From a Letter to Dr. Middleton, 1749

### "Heart Religion" and Contemporary Thought

#### Wesley's *Orthokardia*

Wesley's vision of Christianity contains an important place for both right belief and right action. But "orthodoxy" and "orthopraxis" do not exhaustively describe what was essential to his vision of Christianity. What is missing is what I term the ortho*kardia* - the right heart.[1] This orthokardia is a vision of Christianity which cannot be conveyed by stressing only beliefs or actions, yet neither is it conveyed by focusing on self-contained inner states or "feelings." Without such a "right heart," there is no Christianity on Wesley's terms.

154

While speculative metaphysics held little allure for Wesley, he did hold an important place for doctrinal formulations which (as the motto for this chapter states) describe the Christian character. These doctrines (always carefully distinguished from "mere opinion"[2]) were once summarized as "repentance, faith and holiness"[3] and in another place were characterized as "original sin, justification by faith and holiness consequent thereon."[4] But as we have seen throughout this study,[5] Wesley never thought that Christianity could be a religion of sheer intellectual assent to a set of disembodied doctrines. Faith-as-assent, while important, could, by itself, only yield the "faith of a devil, a train of ideas in the head."

Similarly, a singular emphasis on "doing," on the active, serving side of the Christian life, did not tell the whole story. Moralistic preaching, with its deadening and joyless prescriptions, was driving people away from Christ and His church. What was needed, according to Wesley, was to put the truths of Christianity into practice in real life in the real world, the world where joy meets despair, where trust meets fear, where love meets hate. It was Wesley's ability to convey the truth of Christianity in the terminology of the heart that made his vision so compelling during his time, and it is this same characteristic which continues to make it relevant, even to our post-modern age.

Wesley's orthokardia cannot, as some would have it, be translated into any easy talk about 'sincerity.' In his *Plain Account of Christian Perfection*, question 12 asks "Does Christian perfection imply any more than sincerity?" To which Wesley answers

> Not if you mean by that word, love filling the heart, expelling pride, anger, desire, self-will; rejoicing evermore, praying without ceasing, and in everything giving thanks. But I doubt, few use sincerity in this

sense.  Therefore, I think the old word ['perfection'] is best.[6]

Wesley's orthokardia is nothing else than an embodiment of the fruit of the Spirit of Galatians 5:22ff, or the living-out of Romans 14:17 where the Kingdom of God is described as righteousness, peace and joy in the Holy Spirit.  The orthokardia is nothing else than what is contained in the Sermon on the Mount, which Wesley saw as "the sum of all true religion laid down in eight particulars."[7]  Such an orientation of the heart obviously needs to be formed by a particular construal of the Gospel, which implies vigorous application of reason and will in a disciplined grappling with theological truth.  But for Wesley, the intellectual and theological components of this task are useful only to the extent that they serve in the process of formation.  The second-order, abstract language of theology is only justified if it serves to enable the correct deployment of the first-order language and behavior associated with such concepts as love, joy and peace.  In hopes of making clear how emotion language is related to the task of theology as Wesley saw it, let us consider some contemporary research into the nature of theological discourse.

**A Contemporary View of Religion and Theology**

George Lindbeck's recent analysis of religion and theology gives us one way of appreciating the important and distinctive contributions of Wesley.  In his book *The Nature of Doctrine*,[8] Lindbeck says that there are three ways of defining a religion.  One can, first of all, differentiate between religions by looking at their cognitive assertions, their belief systems.  This tends to lead to a once-and-for-all defining of absolute religious truth as embodied in propositions.

Lindbeck's second way of looking at religion is to judge them on the basis of how well they express the (presumed) single religious impulse of humanity. All humans are seen as having certain in-built capacities which are expressed in relatively better or worse ways by the various religions. On this view, there is one universal "experience" which is "expressed" in a variety of ways.

Lindbeck's third understanding of religion is defined along cultural-linguistic lines. This view does not define religion by doctrine, neither does it assume that all religions are trying to "express" the same thing. Lindbeck's third option takes seriously the real differences between religious communities and it defines religion as a set of linguistic and behavioral practices.

In such a scheme, it might be tempting to classify all thinkers who emphasize the religious affections as falling into the second of Lindbeck's categories, where he places the existentialists who speak about a universal "depth-dimension" uncovered in certain experiences of "authenticity." But instead, the affection-centered views of people like Wesley and Edwards are best placed in Lindbeck's third category, the cultural-linguistic.

For Wesley, Christianity is not seen as the welling-up of an in-built instinct, it is a disciplined form of life distinguished by a certain pattern of affectivity. If belief does not engender a specific set of affections, which in turn lead to certain behaviors in the world, then the Gospel has not been understood. Opposing both rationalism (Christianity as assent to correct beliefs) and so-called pietism (Christianity as a matter of felt experience), Wesley aimed to show that theological integrity and a rich emotional life are not inconsistent with each other. His aim was, in fact, to show that these two require each other.

Lindbeck shows that on this cultural-linguistic understanding of religion, theology functions as a "grammar" for the linguistic and behavioral acts which define the Christian culture. A grammar in a language is an abstract, second-order set of rules which governs the first-order language of every day life. A grammar does not exist so that people speak nothing but the rules of grammar. Instead, a grammar exists so that all of the normal first-order concerns of life may be expressed meaningfully.

Similarly, Christian theology - as abstract, second-order "grammar" - does not seek to make all people fluent in theological discourse. Instead, theology is to provide the paradigm, the defining vision, of the essential features of the Christian life, including speech, actions and emotions. Theology, then, has the role of providing the guidelines for behavior - linguistic and otherwise - in such a way that the behavior of the people in the believing community can be made consistent with the Christian vision of life. Just as one can speak grammatically without knowing what a direct object or a gerund is, one can also behave in a Christian manner without knowing what the doctrine of atonement is about or to what "ecclesiology" refers.[9] The goal of the properly lived Christian life is not to have an unshakeable grasp of the meta-language of theology. The goal of the Christian life is to grasp properly, and use, the first-order language of faith, hope and love, which implies attending to the right objects and performing the right actions.

This understanding of religion and theology painted by Lindbeck helps us to see the importance of Wesley's heart-centered vision of Christianity for us today. His theology, expressed in terms of the heart, allows for direct application to real life. His "plain words for plain people" allowed the simple message of the Gospel to change hearts and lives without requiring the believer to be a post-graduate student in theology. His transparent grammar showed that the challenging part of Christianity is not understanding what Christian doctrine states. The challenging part of Christianity is in living a life of faith working through love.

## Experience, Emotion and Theology

The 1984 *Book of Discipline* of the United Methodist Church states that "Experience is to the individual as tradition is to the church."[10] This is true to Wesley's position regarding the term "experience" in its broadest connotations. As Frank Baker has put it, "experience" for Wesley "meant not an instinctive feeling for a thing's rightness, but the findings of a series of tests."[11] Experience can confirm doctrine but not be the source of it.

But seeing that "experience" in this sense plays only a limited role in Wesley's theology in no way vitiates his deserved reputation for emphasizing the concrete lived experience of the Christian. While he often used "experience" in loose and generous ways, this usage usually found more specific expression in concrete discussion of the religious affections and their objects. For Wesley, the Gospel that is distilled from Scripture, interpreted by the Fathers and understood by reason is nothing other than this: that we are to love as we have been loved, and that this love is not a mere sensation or feeling. This love entails attending to the objects which God points us to and desiring the things which God would have us desire. It is a fundamental disposition, a graced habit of intention, which both targets and receives God. It is the way to holiness and thus to happiness.

By emphasizing the love, joy and peace of holiness as the goals of life - his orthokardia - Wesley showed that the affections were much more than what they are commonly regarded to be, that is, inner states which are a source of error and confusion or which only confound the so-called "higher" faculties of reason and understanding. Wesley showed that if the seeker after truth was not humbly filled with love and joy about what God had done for him or her, then the Gospel message had not really been heard and Christianity had not yet taken root in that person's life. He knew that such a position made him somewhat vulnerable to the charge of "enthusiasm" or "emotionalism." But his reading of the Gospel convinced him that this was a risk that all Christians had to run.

Much contemporary theologizing tends to avoid discussing the emotional life in the theological context, seeing it as too embarrassing and "pietistic." If the existence of individual Christians is discussed at all, it is usually by using the more all-encompassing term "experience" instead of "emotion." But the work of people like Lindbeck and Wayne Proudfoot[12] (and also the liberationists in a different way) show that there is no neutral, true-for-all-times-and-places "experience" to which a decisive appeal can be made. It is, therefore, both more true to Wesley *and* more in line with current "post-modern" thinking[13] to talk about the contingent pattern of affectivity being formed in any particular community (e.g., pride and greed in a wealthy suburb; envy and hatred in a barrio, etc.) than to talk about one universal "experience" or one necessarily present "heart" in all of us (as some romantics would have it). There is nothing "inside" of us that we, in our God-given freedom, have not (consciously or otherwise) allowed to take root there. We will either nurture and grow the fruit of the Spirit or the fruit of the spirits of this world. We need a pattern for our inner *formation* (not merely a guide for inner *discovery*) and Wesley's theology, couched in terms of the affections, can provide that.

### The Critical Questions Reconsidered

We have come now to the point of giving specific and direct answers to the critical questions which have been shaping our study of Wesley's thought from the very beginning. Let us, then, subject his views to an examination regarding the role that reason plays in his affectional theology, the extent to which he acknowledges (and defends against) self-deception as a problem of the spiritual life and the extent to which his understanding of the affections promotes a solipsistic or self-absorbed faith.

**Reason and the Affections**

There are several senses to the question of whether or not Wesley's views were "rational." In one sense, we might ask about the relations between affectivity and the "mind" or "reason." A broader sense of the question might be phrased "Does Wesley's position regarding the affections paint a complete, coherent picture, does it show a comprehensible logic?"

In answer to the first question, we have seen over and over again that Wesley holds a high regard for reasoning which has been illumined by grace. The religious affections work in concert with the reflective mind, not against it.[14] Wesley never fell into the trap that ensnared the pietism of Zinzendorf which "failed to keep spiritual vitality and intellectual vigor in proper balance."[15] Unaided human reason, guided by a corrupt heart, could in no way understand, much less explain, the Gospel as revealed in Scripture and interpreted by the fathers of the Church. But *without* reason there could be no properly religious affections, as seen, for example, in his comment on James 1:5 where he talks about the "affections of the mind" or in his note on Romans 10:2 where he says that zeal must be linked to knowledge. In this sense Wesley helps us to see that the common split between reason and emotion needs to be sublated. Wesley showed that being a Christian entails neither a strict "rationalist" position (which denigrates anything "emotional") nor the extremes of "enthusiasm" (where the emphasis is on "feeling" and emotions undisciplined by Biblically informed thinking).

A second way of asking about the rationality of Wesley's conception of the affections is the broader question of the coherence or logic of his views. The answer to this question has been shown through Wesley's constant emphasis on the patterning, forming and disciplining of the affections. This is seen in the biblical commentaries, his sermons, especially on the witness of the Spirit, as well as throughout his abridgement of Edwards's *Treatise*. The truly gracious affections are *not* random and ineffable feeling-states but are predictable and regular patterns of behavior. Some recent commentators on Wesley's theology, have, however, not always made clear this distinction.

Theodore Runyon, in a plenary address given to the theological consultation celebrating the Bicentennial of American Methodism, betrayed a common confusion on this question. After stating that "experience" for Wesley is not an entirely "subjective" thing he goes on to state that

> When Wesley insists that this change in the heart is the *sine qua non* of genuine religion, he is not concerned about an emotion. He is not insisting that persons should feel a certain way.[16]

Here we see an attempt to rescue Wesley from appearing too emotional. But we have seen that the affections *are* crucial for Wesley and to deny this violates the very fabric of his thought. Wesley's theology translated out of the language of the affections ceases to be his theology. What Runyon has not done is make the distinction between *feeling* an emotion and *having* an emotion. This distinction is implied in Wesley's downplaying of conscious sensation (feeling) while at the same time emphasizing the affections (or emotions). Let us consider a common sense example to understand what is at stake in this distinction between feeling and emotion.

One can speak of a man loving his wife even if the man is asleep. While sleeping, he does not cease to love his wife even though he is not (while asleep) constantly experiencing sensations or feelings of love for her. This is to say that love, and other emotions, are more than feelings or sensations. They are standing dispositions which characterize a person over time. Wesley was struggling to make a distinction like this, but the conceptual tools were not available for him to do so.[17] We must be careful, when trying to understand Wesley, not to throw out the emotional life of the heart while we justifiably guard against an over-emphasis on felt sensation.

A similar problem arises in John Deschner's analysis of *Wesley's Christology*.[18] In the 1985 "Foreword" to this book, Deschner states clearly the importance and contemporary relevance of Wesley's soteriological formulations. Deschner points out that, for Wesley, salvation is a "present thing" and that the mind of Christ

> takes form today in the renewed 'affections' of the believer's heart--those affections which constitute the presence in the forgiven sinner of the progressively recovered image of God....*this* is the christological foundation of the Methodist tradition and the main emphasis in any Methodist contribution to the ecumenical recovery of the wholeness of the apostolic faith.[19]

But after this glowing endorsement of Wesley's emphasis on the affections in the Preface, later, in the body of the text, Deschner launches a critique of Wesley which betrays a misunderstanding of Wesley's conception of the affections. Part of Deschner's critique of Wesley is that the moral law given in the Old Testament retains a "semi-independence from Christ."[20] Even when it is understood that for Wesley love is the sum of the law, Deschner still objects that

[Wesley] means by love, not primarily participation in the being of Christ's love, but an inherent 'temper,' 'affection' or 'intention' in man, himself....the independence of the love demanded from the holiness of Christ's active obedience is the root of a far-reaching question about the justice of man's final justification.[21]

Deschner is concerned that Wesley's understanding of holiness is too easily translated into a legalistic moralism, depending on subjective feelings and one's own will to get to heaven. That this understanding was indeed adopted by some of Wesley's followers (especially in the nineteenth century) is undeniable, but it is not fair to accuse Wesley of this. On this point, Deschner seems to have seen Schleiermacher when he looked at Wesley, which is understandable since Deschner originally wrote his book as a dissertation under the direction of Karl Barth. The key words in the above quote which betray Deschner's misunderstanding of Wesley's view of the affections are "inherent" and "independence."

We have seen that for Wesley the affections are not "inherent" and "independent," but are causally dependent on targeting the "things of God," taking the Gospel as the object of our attention, centering our hearts and minds on what God has done for us. We love, not because we have some "inherent" and "independent" principle inside of us. We love because God first loved us. This is no Schleiermacherian in-built "feeling of absolute dependence," it is a contingent pattern of affectivity, it is the result of being "formed in the Christian rule."[22] Holiness is not a question of autonomous willing guided by inherent principles or spontaneous and unpredictable up-wellings of intense feeling, it is "righteousness, joy and peace *in the Holy Ghost.*"[23]

The gracious affections, then, are not mere feelings but are analyzable dispositions which (animated in the synergism of the Holy Spirit and the human spirit) pattern and orient the self. God's atoning work is the object of these affections and (through the confirmation and strengthening of the sacramental ministry of the church) they become dispositions to behave, dispositions to do those works of love and mercy which the compassionate heart perceives to be needed. The transitive and dispositional nature of the affections is seen consistently throughout Wesley's works and this definite pattern of logical connections outside of the self allows us to judge Wesley's conception of the religious affections rational in the larger sense.

A third way of approaching the question of the rationality of emotions is to ask the question: Does the object under consideration justify the emotion elicited? This question cannot be answered in the abstract but only within a particular context in a particular community. Fear of unicorns is irrational in societies which consider such beasts non-existent. Love of God is irrational if one believes that God does not exist. Unbelievers, therefore, might find Wesley's whole scheme to be irrational because of their very unbelief in God. But since, presumably, unbelievers would find *any* portrayal of Christian Theology to be irrational, their rejection of Wesley's theology is not a telling critique of his affection-centered theology.[24]

### The Affections, Self-Deception and Society

In his *The Making of the English Working Class*, E.P. Thompson called Methodism "a ritualized form of psychic masturbation."[25] In point of fact, Wesley did once write a pamphlet on the very subject of "Onanism".[26] A quote from Wesley is also listed in the *Oxford English Dictionary* under the listing for the word "Enthusiast."[27] But in both the pamphlet and the quote in the *O.E.D.*, Wesley not only recognizes the possibility and reality of self-manipulation, but he also warns against it in both the sexual and the spiritual realm. This vigilance against "curving in on oneself" (to use Luther's phrase) is never more apparent than when Wesley speaks about the affections.

As we have seen, Wesley does not recommend a religion of sheer undifferentiated feeling. What makes an affection Christian (or "religious" or "gracious") is the object which engenders it. To be specific, the genuine religious affections take as their object the story of what God has done for us in Christ. Having such a "descriptive" object as the target of our affections is admittedly different than having them take a spatio-temporal object like a tree or a human being.[28] This difference can open-up another possibility for delusion, namely taking the *wrong* description of God as the object of the affections. But Wesley's constant insistence on the normative nature of Scripture (interpreted by the Church) as the main source for our understanding of God is another very strong check against tailoring our religion to our own desires.

Since our focus in this work has been on what Wesley *said* in his published works about the affections, we have not considered what shape the actual *practice* of his own ministry took in forming these affections in his scattered flocks. But it must not be forgotten, especially when considering this problem of self-deception, that one of the most important instruments that Wesley used for deepening the faith, hope and love of believers was the class meeting. Wesley was not one to recommend lonely mountaintop contemplation, for he knew too well the human heart's propensity for deceit. Wesley was constantly forming new believers into classes, societies and bands where the Christians could examine each other and openly and honestly share with each other the course of their spiritual struggles. Seeking "feedback" and direction from others was more the norm for the Methodist movement than the exception. Wesley's emphasis on the social nature of the

Christian life and the constant need to guard against self-deception - in other words, the need for "accountable discipleship" - has been very helpfully expounded in David Lowes Watson's book *The Early Methodist Class Meeting*.[29]

We have also seen that having a Christian "heart" logically entails the doing of certain actions in the world, summarized briefly as "loving your neighbor."[30] A right heart requires right works just as doing works Christianly requires a right heart. If Wesley had said that being a Christian meant only experiencing certain positive feelings, like pleasure, then he would be an appropriate patron saint of the "me generation." But Wesley's understanding of Christianity called for self-denial, taking up one's cross and following after Christ. The love, joy and peace of this life are all marked by humility and the "filial fear" of offending God, and there is a continuing need for "The Repentance of Believers" (sermon number 14).

Wesley placed true religion in the realm of the affections, but to understand correctly what he means by this is to see that the grammar of the religious affections bursts open the self in two different ways. At their genesis, the affections are formed by attending to the work of Christ, which is not something self-generated but is something which comes to us as proclamation. After grace has thus led us to faith, we are naturally led to do the "works of mercy" by the love of God and neighbor which has grown within us. Thus the affections have not only their genesis outside of the self, but their *telos* as well.[31] On this understanding, then, Wesley escapes the critique of "religion as inwardness" which Dietrich Bonhoeffer levels in his writings.[32] There is no such thing as a solitary Christian for Wesley, and the Christian that does no works is no Christian at all. In The "Large Minutes" of the Methodist conference, the purpose of the group is set out as propagating scriptural holiness *and* reforming the nation, *not* one or the other.[33]

We see in all of this, then, the answer not just to the question of self-deception as a spiritual problem, but also to the third critical question about an emphasis on the affections possibly fostering an extreme individualism. Doing works in society is ingredient in having a religious affection. Wesley's observation that "there can be no holiness but social holiness" is entirely consistent with his emphasis on the religious affections.

Moreover, Wesley's discussions of the affections, which carefully balance feeling, object and disposition, shed light on a paradox of which most of us are aware. The paradox I refer to is the fact that many of our most deeply held convictions are guarded by an outward calm, an apparent serenity, rather than strong displays of feeling. These convictions seem somehow too important to display in an exuberant way. I think this is so because the dispositional nature of our emotions is seen most clearly in our strongest affections. The dispositional nature of our religious beliefs is so clear that to try to express them completely through bursts of feeling is clearly futile. Feeling just cannot be substituted for action. Wesley realized that what makes religious language so hard to speak is that it is an idiom which demands much of the speaker. The "meaning" of our religious discourse is not found in a feeling, but in the actions which make-up our lives.[34]

Freud and Marx showed that history - both personal and societal - can distort what we call "reason." Wittgenstein went beyond these insights and showed that in fact "reason" *required* history, i.e., a pre-existing community of shared language and practice. Wittgenstein's insights into reason can be found *mutatis mutandis* in Wesley's insights into the religious affections. The affections require a society, a community, for both their formation and their expression. The church conveys the story of God's action and provides the liturgical means for forming the affections which the story engenders. And the church and the wider community are the arena for the actions to which the affections dispose the believers. The religious affections for Wesley were fundamentally relational.

## Practical Theology in the Post-Modern World

### "Practical" Theology

Many Christians, ministers and laypeople alike, are growing tired of hearing theology dissolved into psychology. There is a growing unease about the secular disciplines setting our Christian agenda for understanding the spiritual life. Wesley's views about the religious affections provide a decisive challenge to the present received wisdom which relegates theology to the task of filling-in the gaps in the theories of therapists.

Wesley's theology differs from that of many modern pastoral psychologizers. Many popularizers, who have filled the pastoral counseling bookshelves with works which promise the translation of Christianity into terms of mental health, are distinguishable from Wesley's style of Christianity in at least two ways. First of all, those who write from a psychological viewpoint tend to focus more on particular *problems* of the emotional life (e.g., inappropriate guilt, uncontrollable anger, etc.). Wesley, in contrast, provides a more fully integrated theology which defines the core of the Gospel proclamation in terms of the heart and thus gives a positive vision for the role of doctrine in the emotional life.

Secondly, at least among some of the popularizers, the "world" tends to be seen as the source of problems for the life of the heart and Christianity is seen primarily as the source of the answers to these problems. At its crudest, this kind of approach paints Christianity as the provider only of consolation, never challenges. For Wesley, however, Christianity does not just provide ointment for our wounds, it also calls us to enter into suffering, patterning our emotions and motivations so that we will not shun the cross in favor of worldly glory, honor and comfort. The Christian life has emotional consolations, but they are not what the world might expect. To ignore this is neither practical nor Christian, and Wesley faced this truth directly and proclaimed it loudly.

There has been much interest of late in the topic of "Practical" Theology. A recent book by that title edited by Don Browning contains a plea (made by James Fowler) for a more affection-centered practical theology,[35] but this plea has not yet been heeded. Indeed, much of the recent work in this "new" field seems to be re-inventing the wheel while over-looking the richness that the Wesleyan heritage has to offer.[36]

The focus of this discipline is not on speculation but on the actual practice of ministry and, more generally, the actual practice of *Christianity*. The recent work done in this field has again emphasized that *systematic* theology is not the only kind of *important* theology. Because of this, we need not feel ashamed about taking someone like Wesley as our theological conversation partner simply because he did not write a "systematic" theology. What is more important than theology being "systematic" is that it be done (as Albert Outler has often pointed-out[37]) *coram Deo* (in the presence of God) and this is what Wesley did. T. S. Eliot once said that poetry is not the assertion that something is true, but the making of that truth more fully real to us. The same should be said of truly practical theology, and Wesley's theology meets this criterion.

Implicit in the thought of Wesley is the judgment that affectivity does not easily fit into the artificial structures of the university or the seminary. Emotion cannot be left exclusively to the province of the psychologist and the pastoral counselor. The theologian must see that the nature of emotion has definite implications for the Christian life and that the Christian story has important implications for the affectional life. Both the theologian of the ivory tower and the counselor concerned solely with "feelings" are left behind in Wesleyan practical theology. Wesley saw that the normative question of theology ("What is Christianity?") *must* be brought together with the counselor's quest for self-knowledge ("How does that make you feel?") if all of the truths of the Gospel are to be embodied. For Wesley, it could never be *either* head or heart, it had to be both/and.

## Wesley's *Orthokardia* in the Post-Modern World

We cannot conclude by saying that there were no unresolved aspects to Wesley's understanding of the religious affections. In one particular way, his thought was an insular expression of the eighteenth century. During that time, Christianity itself was not a question for an English clergyman. There was for Wesley little concern for many of the very real issues of inter-religious dialogue which our age of religious pluralism presents to us. If he had lived today, he might very well have broadened-out his concerns with religious experience into a cross-cultural study as someone like Rudolf Otto did. But in any case, we cannot look to Wesley for this.

Many things also still need to be explored about Wesley's theology which did not receive scrutiny in this analysis of Wesley's thought, such as the precise nature of the "object" of faith (in other words, Wesley's conception of God, the Trinity, Jesus). Also unanswered in this work is the specific form which a Wesleyan ethic should take today - what *kinds* of actions should we be doing today based on the love of God and neighbor. These are legitimate questions but beyond the scope of the present study.

What I have shown in the previous pages is that Wesley's language about the religious affections is coherent and intellectually defensible *vis a vis* some of the more pressing concerns of modern theology. Though a man of his day in many ways, his insights about the affections are enduring. His personal engagement with the world as preacher, church leader, spiritual guide, controversialist and all the rest lead him to emphasize (and sometimes over-emphasize) certain aspects of his understanding of the affections depending on the circumstances, and this, more often than not, did leave him open to misinterpretation. To the enthusiast, he sounded like a rationalist. To the rationalist, he sounded like an enthusiast. To the quietist caught-up in the "inner" life, he would emphasize the "outer" life and sound like an activist. To the philosopher he would emphasize the supernatural. To the mystic, he would emphasize the natural. This shifting of his rhetorical weight sometimes left him off balance (seen, for example, in his radical rejection of the doctrinal elements of the faith when in polemical exchange with his Calvinist opponents). But when taken on the whole, his position is not only internally coherent, but a rewarding source of insight that is still relevant to theological concerns.

Through focusing on that feature of Wesley's theology which is often regarded as the most individualistic, subjective and "inner" - his emphasis on the religious affections - we have seen that even this aspect of his theology is fundamentally relational. He has shown through his reflections on human experience and the Christian faith that a certain pattern of affectivity must be present if Christianity is to be said to exist. The emotions cannot be left to the psychologist, the theologian must proclaim to the world that the emotional realm is the province of every Christian *qua* believer.

The Argentinian Methodist Jose Miguez Bonino in his influential *Doing Theology in a Revolutionary Situation* states that for Liberation Theology, "*Orthopraxis*, rather than orthodoxy, becomes the criterion for theology."[38] Similar sentiments are expressed by Black theologians as well as

Feminist thinkers.[39] Such approaches, in their rejection of the sufficiency of either abstract doctrine or mystical experiences for defining the true nature of Christianity, will get a sympathetic hearing among the followers of Wesley. However, those who *oppose* praxis to the "interior" life are in need of correction. People like Herbert Marcuse, writing on aesthetics, have shown that treating subjectivity as a "bourgeois" notion, as the classical Marxists do, is historically questionable and even damaging to the goal of social reform.[40] Marcuse recognizes that there is a mutually generative relationship between the "inner" and the "outer" and to have one we must have the other. Such "new" insights from the "critical school" can serve only to reinforce Wesley's rigorous theological apprehension of the rational and social nature of affectivity.

If Wesley's vision of true "heart religion" were taken seriously today it would lead to anything but self-centered navel-gazing. It would lead to an explosion of creative Christian action unprecedented in our time. The "vital piety" which Wesley described could once again, as it did in his time, reform the church and the world.

1. Theodore Runyon has also shown the need for a third "ortho" term in describing Wesley's theology. In his "A New Look at 'Experience'" (*Drew Gateway* Fall 1987, 44-55, based on a presentation at the 1984 Minister's Week of Emory University) he uses the phrase "orthopathy," though his exposition does not deal explicitly with issues of object-centeredness and how feelings differ from emotions. On this latter issue, see below pages 162f and note 17.

2. E.g., *Journal*, III, 534; IV, 419; *Letters* IV, 146; V225-29; VI, 28; Jackson's edition of Wesley's *Works*, VIII, 46-49, 67, 472; IX, 174. These references were cited in Outler's *John Wesley* (New York: Oxford University Press, 1964) 120.

3. See "The Principles of a Methodist Farther Explained," Jackson's edition of Wesley's *Works*, volume VIII, 472.

4. *Letters* volume 4, 146.

5. Especially in Chapter 5 in the section titled "What Christianity is and What it is not."

6. London: Epworth, 1983, 74.

7. The eight points, of course, are the beatitudes: *poverty of spirit, mourning* and *meekness* are explained in terms of humility and repentance; *hungering and thirsting after righteousness* is seen as the desire for the life of the Spirit; *mercy* is translated into terms of love which is exposited by reference to 1 Corinthians 13; and his descriptions of being *pure in heart,* being a *peacemaker* and being *persecuted for righteousness sake* finish the picture of a religion of the heart which takes its origin in God and leads to joyful and sacrificial service.

8. Philadelphia: Westminster Press, 1984

9. For more about Lindbeck's theory and its importance see my "Finding a Place for Emotions in Theology" in the *Christian Century,* (April 29, 1987) and Mark Horst's Review of Lindbeck's book in *Quarterly Review* (volume 8, number 1, Spring 1988), 89-97. For an analysis of religious emotion which is congruent with the views of Lindbeck - showing it to be dependent on concepts and beliefs which are provided by the cultural context - see Wayne Proudfoot's *Religious Experience* (Berkeley: University of California Press, 1985).

10. Page 80.

11. *John Wesley and the Church of England* (Nashville: Abingdon, 1970) 24.

12. See note number 9 above.

13. That is, those views which deny the enlightenment emphasis on a univocal reason which can solve all problems.

14. See above, 80ff.

15. Gerald R. Cragg *The Church and the Age of Reason* (Penquin Books, 1960) 104.

16. "What is Methodism's Theological Contribution Today?" in *Wesleyan Theology Today* (Nashville: Kingswood Books, 1985), p. 12.

17. See sermon 41 "Wandering Thoughts" III, 7: "It follows that none of these wandering thoughts...are inconsistent with perfect love. Indeed if they were, then not only sharp pain, but sleep itself would be inconsistent with it." (134) Theodore W. Jennings, Jr. has obviously not grasped this distinction between feelings and emotions when he points to the fluctuations in Wesley's own spiritual life and concludes

that "Neither before [Aldersgate] nor after did Wesley find it possible to 'love' the God he so vigorously served." (*Quarterly Review* Vol. 8, No. 3, Fall 1988, 19.) See above, especially pp. 60-64 and 118-120. Two of the most recent discussions of the distinction between feeling an emotion and having one are found in *Affectivity* by James Brown (Washington D.C.: University Press of America, 1982) and *Emotion* by William Lyons (Cambridge: Cambridge University Press, 1980).

18. (Dallas: S.M.U. Press, 1985). Quotations are from this edition though this work has also recently been re-issued by Zondervan.

19. Pages xvi-xvii.

20. 106. See also 107-8; 140-141; 154ff.; 180; 193f.

21. 106.

22. See above, 116.

23. Romans 14:17, one of Wesley's favorite descriptions of the Kingdom of God. Geoffrey Wainwright also criticizes Deschner for denying that holiness is achieved on Wesley's terms by "participating in Christ," though Wainwright does so by emphasizing Wesley's sacramental views. I agree with Wainwright's sacramental point, but I think Deschner's more fundamental confusion lies in his understanding of Wesley's view of the affections. See Wainwright's review of Deschner's book in *Perkins Journal* (volume 39, number 2, April 1986), 55-56.

On the question of Wesley's understanding of the law, see also Leander Keck's *Paul and His Letters* (Philadelphia: Fortress, 1979) and Krister Stendahl's *Paul Among Jews and Gentiles* (Philadelphia: Fortress, 1976) for discussions of Paul's understanding of the law. It seems that if one accepts the analysis of Paul's views of the law as set forth by Keck and Stendahl (i.e., that the law itself is not bad, but that it can not bring about what only faith can do) then Wesley's claims that the "law is established through faith" and that "faith is the handmaid to love" (see sermons 35 and 36, especially *Sermons* volume II, 38) are perhaps more Pauline than some Reformation understandings.

24. For a discussion of how "reason" requires a specific community, see the work of Alasdair MacIntyre, especially *Whose Justice? Which Rationality?* (Notre Dame: Notre Dame Press, 1988).

25. (New York: 1966) 368.

26. "Thoughts on the Sin of Onan" (London: 1767).

27. Volume 1 of the 2 volume edition, 876.

28. On emotions taking descriptive objects, see John Berntsen's "Christian Affections and the Catechumenate," *Worship*, volume 52, 1978, and Calhoun and Solomon, eds., *What is an Emotion?* (New York: Oxford University Press, 1984) for more on the relationship between emotion and belief.

29. (Nashville: Discipleship Resources, 1985). For two contemporary secular discussions of how a select "competent community" is necessary for effective interpretation, discussion and formation, see Wayne Booth's *The Dogma of Modern Assent* (Chicago: University of Chicago Press, 1974) and Hans Georg Gadamer's *Truth and Method* (New York: Continuum, 1975).

30. See above, 78ff; 120ff.

31. On the subtle temptation to target our feelings instead of targeting God, see C.S. Lewis' *The Screwtape Letters*, letter number 6.

32. E.g. *Letters and Papers from Prison*, letter of July 8, 1944.

33. Jackson *Works*, volume 8, 299.

34. On this theme, see Don E. Saliers, *The Soul in Paraphrase: Prayer and the Religious Affections* (New York: Seabury Press, 1980) especially 112ff. Saliers says that living out of certain emotions means more than having intense feelings but entails taking-up a way of life (113). For a criticism of substituting feeling for action, see Jean-Paul Sartre's *The Emotions: Outline of a Theory* (New York: Philosophical Library, 1948). While Sartre has made a profound insight into some types of emotional experience, he unfortunately over-generalizes and can see no positive role for emotion, terming all emotion a degradation of consciousness.

35. *Practical Theology* (San Francisco: Harper and Row, 1983) 160-161.

36. See Edward Farley's *Theologia* (Philadelphia: Fortress Press, 1983) for a discussion of theological education in the modern era which documents the need for a more unified emphasis on sapiential knowledge instead of training the minister to be the master of a set of specialized sciences or, even worse, a "professional." Neither Farley's book nor Fortress Press's latest entry into this field (*Formation and Reflection: The Promise of Practical Theology*, 1987), however, contain a single reference to the thought of John Wesley. Even when Methodist-related thinkers discussed the issue of practical

theology with a well-known theologian [*Hope for the Church: Moltmann in Dialogue with Practical Theology*, Runyon, ed. (Nashville: Abingdon, 1979)] Wesley's thought never makes an appearance.

37. See, for example, *Quarterly Review*, volume 8, number 2, Summer, 1988, 8.

38. Philadelphia: Fortress, 1975, 21.

39. See, for example, Cornel West's *Prophesy Deliverance!* (Philadelphia: Westminster Press, 1982) and the essays by Rosemary Radford Ruether and Elizabeth Schussler Fiorenza in Judith Weidman's (editor) *Christian Feminism* (San Francisco: Harper and Row, 1984).

40. See *The Aesthetic Dimension* (Boston: Beacon, 1978) 1-21.

# SELECT BIBLIOGRAPHY

## Primary Sources

*The Works of The Rev. John Wesley*, 3rd ed., ed. Thomas Jackson. 14 volumes. (London: Wesleyan-Methodist Book Room, 1829-31). Reprinted, (Grand Rapids: Zondervan Publishing House, 1958); (Grand Rapids: Baker Book House, 1979). Abbreviated as Jackson *Works*.

*The Journal of John Wesley*, ed. Nehemiah Curnock. 8 volumes (London: Robert Cully, 1909-1916) Reprinted, (London: Epworth Press, 1938). Abbreviated as *Journal*.

*The Letters of John Wesley*, ed. John Telford. 8 volumes (London: Epworth Press, 1931).

*Wesley's Standard Sermons*, ed. Edward H. Sugden. 2 volumes, reprinted, (London: Epworth Press, 1921; 5th ed., 1961)

*Explanatory Notes Upon the New Testament* (London: William Bowyer, 1755) Reprinted (London: Epworth Press, 1976). Abbreviated as N.T. *Notes*.

*Explanatory Notes Upon the Old Testament* (Bristol: William Pine, 1765) Reprinted (Salem: Schmul, 1975). Abbreviated as O.T. *Notes*.

*The Oxford Edition of the Works of John Wesley*, gen. ed. Frank Baker, 4 volumes (Oxford: Clarendon Press, 1975-1983).

*Volume 7*: *A Collection of Hymns for the Use of the People Called Methodists*, ed. Franz Hildebrandt, *et al*, (1983).

*Volume 11*: *The Appeals to Men of Reason and Religion and Certain Related Open Letters*, ed. Gerald R. Cragg (1975).

*Volume 25*: *Letters I, 1721-1739*, ed. Frank Baker (1980).

*Volume 26*: *Letters II, 1740-1755*, ed. Frank Baker (1982).

*The Works of John Wesley* (Nashville: Abingdon)

*Volume 1: Sermons 1-33*, ed. Albert C. Outler (1984).

*Volume 2: Sermons 34-70*, ed. Albert C. Outler (1985).

*Volume 3: Sermons 71-114*, ed. Albert C. Outler (1986).

*Volume 4: Sermons 115-151*, ed. Albert C. Outler (1987).

### Secondary Sources

Abraham, William J., "The Concept of Inspiration in the Classical Wesleyan Tradition" in Kinghorn, ed., *A Celebration of Ministry* (Wilmore: Francis Asbury, 1982).

Arnott, Felix R., "Anglicanism in the Seventeenth Century" in *Anglicanism*, More and Cross, eds., (N.Y.: The Macmillan Company).

Augustine, *On Christian Doctrine* (Indianapolis: Bobbs-Merrill, 1958).

Ayling, Stanley, *John Wesley* (Nashville: Abingdon, 1979).

Baker, Frank, "The Beginnings of American Methodism," in *Methodist History*, volume 2, number 1 (October 1963) 1-15.

_____, *John Wesley and the Church of England* (Nashville: Abingdon, 1970).

_____, "A Study of John Wesley's Readings" in the *London Quarterly and Holborn Review* 168 (1943), pages 140-145; 234-242.

_____, ed., *A Union Catalogue of the Publications of John and Charles Wesley* (Durham: Duke University, 1966).

Barr, James, *The Semantics of Biblical Language* (Oxford: Oxford University Press, 1961).

Becker, C. L., *The Heavenly City of the Eighteenth Century Philosophers* (New Haven: Yale University Press, 1932).

Bence, Clarence L., "John Wesley's Teleological Hermeneutic," Ph.D. dissertation, Emory University, 1980.

Benner, Forest T., "The Immediate Antecedents of the Wesleyan Doctrine of the Witness of the Spirit," Ph.D. dissertation, 1966).

Berntsen, John, "Christian Affections and the Catechumenate" in *Worship* volume 52, 1978, 194-210.

Blankenship, Paul F., "The Significance of John Wesley's Abridgement of the Thirty-Nine Articles as Seen from his Deletions," in *Methodist History* volume 2, number 3 (April 1964), 35-47.

Bonhoeffer, Dietrich, *Letters and Papers from Prison* (New York: Macmillan, 1972).

Booth, Wayne, *The Dogma of Modern Assent* (Chicago: University of Chicago Press, 1974).

Boshears, Onva K., "John Wesley, the Bookman: A Study of His Reading Interests in the Eighteenth Century" Ph.D. dissertation, University of Michigan, 1972.

Brantley, Richard E., *Locke, Wesley, and the Method of English Romanticism* (Gainesville: University of Florida Press, 1984).

Brown, Dale, *Understanding Pietism* (Grand Rapids: Eerdman's, 1978).

Brown, James, *Affectivity* (Washington, D.C.: University Press of America, 1982).

Burtner, R. W., and Chiles, R. E., eds., *A Compend of Wesley's Theology* (New York: Abingdon, 1954).

Campbell, Ted, "John Wesley's Conceptions and Uses of Christian Antiquity," Ph.D. dissertation, S.M.U., 1984.

Cannon, William R., "John Wesley's Doctrine of Sanctification and Perfection" in *Mennonite Quarterly Review* 35 (1961), 91-95.

_____, "Salvation in the Theology of John Wesley" in *Methodist History* volume 9, number 1 (October 1970) 3-12.

_____, *The Theology of John Wesley* (New York: Abingdon, 1946).

Casto, Robert Michael, "Exegetical Method in John Wesley's *Explanatory Notes Upon the Old Testament*: A Description of his Approach, Use of Sources, and Practice," Ph.D. dissertation, Duke University, 1977.

Cell, George C., *The Rediscovery of John Wesley* (New York: Henry Holt and Co., 1935).

Cherry, Charles Conrad, *The Theology of Jonathan Edwards*: *A Reappraisal* (Garden City: Anchor Book, 1966).

Chilcote, Paul Wesley, "The Women Pioneers of Early Methodism" in *Wesleyan Theology Today* (Nashville: Kingswood, 1985) 180-184.

Clapper, Gregory S., "Finding a Place for Emotions in Christian Theology" in *Christian Century* (April 29, 1987).

_____, "Relations Between Theology and Spirituality: Kierkegaard's Model" in *Studies in Formative Spirituality* volume IX, number 2 (May 1988), 161-167.

_____, "'True Religion' and the Affections: A Study of John Wesley's Abridgement of Jonathan Edwards' *Treatise on Religious Affections*" in *Wesleyan Theology Today* (Nashville: Kingswood, 1985), 416-423.

Clebsch, William A., "The Sensible Spirituality of Jonathan Edwards," in his *American Religious Thought*: *A History* (Chicago: University of Chicago Press, 1973), 11-56.

Cragg, Gerald R., *The Church and the Age of Reason 1648-1789* (Harmondsworth: Penquin, 1960).

_____, *Reason and Authority in the Eighteenth Century* (Cambridge: Cambridge University Press, 1964).

Davies, Rupert and Rupp, Gordon, eds., *A History of the Methodist Church in Great Britain* (London: Epworth Press, 1965) 2 volumes.

Delattre, Roland A., *Beauty and Sensibility in the Thought of Jonathan Edwards: An Essay in Aesthetics and Theological Ethics* (New York: Yale University Press, 1968).

Deschner, John, *Wesley's Christology* (Dallas: S.M.U. Press, 1985).

Dreyer, Frederick, "Faith and Experience in the Thought of John Wesley," in *The American Historical Review*, volume 88, Number 1 (February 1982), 12-30.

Edwards, Jonathan, *Works*, general editor, John E. Smith (New Haven: Yale University Press, 1957--).
Volume 1, *Freedom of the Will*, ed. Paul Ramsey, (1957).
Volume 2, *Religious Affections*, ed. John E. Smith, (1959).
Volume 3, *Original Sin*, ed. Clyde A. Holbrook, (1970).
Volume 4, *The Great Awakening*, ed. C. C. Goen, (1972).
Volume 5, *Apocalyptic Writings*, ed. Stephen J. Stein, (1977).
Volume 6, *Scientific and Philosophic Writings*, ed. Wallace E. Anderson, (1980).

Erdt, Terence, "The Calvinist Psychology of the Heart and the 'Sense' of Jonathan Edwards" in *Early American Literature*, volume 13, number 2, (1978), 165-180.

_____, *Jonathan Edwards: Art and the Sense of the Heart* (Amherst: Univ. of Mass. Press, 1980).

Farley, Edward, *Theologia* (Philadelphia: Fortress, 1983).

Fiering, Norman, *Jonathan Edwards' Moral Thought and Its British Context* (Chapel Hill: Univ. of North Carolina Press, 1981).

Frei, Hans, *The Eclipse of the Biblical Narrative* (New Haven: Yale University Press, 1974).

Gadamer, Hans Georg, *Truth and Method* (New York: Continuum, 1975).

Green, Richard, *The Works of John and Charles Wesley* (London: C.H. Kelly, 1896).

Hall, Thor, "The Christian's Life: Wesley's Alternative to Luther and Calvin" in *Duke Divinity School Bulletin* volume 28, number 2 (May 1963), 111-126.

Heitzenrater, Richard, *The Elusive Mr. Wesley*, 2 volumes (Nashville: Abingdon, 1984).

Herbert, T.W., *John Wesley as Editor and Author* (Princeton: Princeton University Press, 1940).

Hildebrandt, Franz, *From Luther to Wesley* (London: Lutterworth, 1951).

Horst, Mark, "Christian Understanding and the Life of Faith in John Wesley's Thought," Ph.D. dissertation, Yale University, 1985.

_____,"Engendering the Community of Faith in an Age of Individualism: A Review of George Lindbeck's *The Nature of Doctrine: Religion and Theology in a Postliberal Age*" in *Quarterly Review* volume 8, number 1 (Spring 1988), 89-97.

_____, "Wholeness and Method in Wesley's Theology," in *Quarterly Review* volume 7, number 2 (Summer 1987), 11-23.

Hynson, Leon O., *To Reform the Nation: Theological Foundations of Wesley's Ethics* (Grand Rapids: Francis Asbury Press, 1984).

Jennings, Theodore W., "John Wesley *Against* Aldersgate" in *Quarterly Review* volume 8, number 3 (Fall 1988) 3-22.

Källstad, Thorvald, *John Wesley and the Bible: A Psychological Perspective* (Stockholm: NYA Bokförlags Aktiebolaget, 1974).

Keck, Leander, *Paul and His Letters* (Philadelphia: Fortress Press, 1979).

Kellet, Norman L., "John Wesley and the Restoration of the Doctrine of the Holy Spirit to the Church of England in the Eighteenth Century" Ph.D. dissertation, 1975).

Kierkegaard, Søren, *Concluding Unscientific Postscript* (Princeton: Princeton University Press, 1941).

Knight, John Allen, "Aspects of Wesley's Theology after 1770," in *Methodist History* volume 6, number 3 (April 1968) 33-42.

Knox, R.A., *Enthusiasm: A Chapter in the History of Religion with Special Reference to the 17th and 18th Centuries* (Oxford: Clarendon Press, 1950).

Lawson, John, *Notes on Wesley's Forty-Four Sermons* (London: Epworth Press, 1946).

Lewis, C. S., *The Screwtape Letters* (West Chicago: Lord and King, 1976).

Lindbeck, George A., *The Nature of Doctrine: Religion and Theology in a Post-liberal Age* (Philadelphia: Westminster, 1984).

Lindstrom, Harald, *Wesley and Sanctification* (London: Epworth Press, 1950).

Lyons, William, *Emotion* (Cambridge: Cambridge University Press, 1980).

MacIntyre, Alasdair, *Whose Justice? Which Rationality?* (Notre Dame: Notre Dame Press, 1988).

Manspeaker, Nancy, *Jonathan Edwards: Bibliographical Synopses* (New York: The Edwin Mellen Press, 1981).

Marcuse, Herbert *The Aesthetic Dimension* (Boston: Beacon, 1978).

Marshall, G.D., "On Being Affected" in *Mind* volume 77 (April 1968), 243-259.

Matthews, Rex D., "Reason, Faith, and Experience in the Thought of John Wesley," a paper presented at the Oxford Institute of Methodist Theological Studies, 1982.

_____, "'With the Eyes of Faith': Spiritual Experience and the Knowledge of God in the Theology of John Wesley" in *Wesleyan Theology Today* (Nashville: Kingswood, 1985), 406-415.

McCarthy, Daryl, "Early Wesleyan Views of Scripture," in *Wesleyan Theological Journal* volume 16, number 2 (Fall 1981) 95-105.

Meeks, M. Douglas, ed., *The Future of the Methodist Theological Traditions* (Nashville: Abingdon, 1985).

Miguez Bonino, Jose, *Doing Theology in a Revolutionary Situation* (Philadelphia: Fortress, 1975).

Miller, Perry, *Jonathan Edwards* (New York: W. Sloane, 1949).

Moore, Robert L., *John Wesley and Authority* (Missoula: Scholar's Press, 1979)

Outler, Albert C., *Evangelism in the Wesleyan Spirit* (Nashville: Tidings, 1971).

_____, ed., *John Wesley* (New York: Oxford University Press, 1964).

_____, "John Wesley as Theologian - Then and Now" in *Methodist History* volume 12, number 4 (July 1974), 63-82.

_____, "Methodism's Theological Heritage: A Study in Perspective" in *Methodism's Destiny in the Ecumenical Age* Paul M. Minus, ed. (New York: Abingdon, 1969), 44-70.

_____, *Theology in the Wesleyan Spirit* (Nashville: Discipleship Resources, 1975).

_____, "Towards a Re-appraisal of John Wesley as a Theologian" in *Perkins Journal* volume 14, number 2 (Winter 1961), 5-14.

Proudfoot, Wayne, *Religious Experience* (Berkeley: University of California Press, 1985).

Ricoeur, Paul, *The Conflict of Interpretations* (Evanston: Northwestern University Press, 1974).

Roberts, Robert C., *Spirituality and Human Emotion* (Grand Rapids: Eerdman's, 1982).

Rogers, Charles A., "The Concept of Prevenient Grace in the Theology of John Wesley," Ph.D. dissertation, Duke University, 1967.

_____, "John Wesley and Jonathan Edwards" in *Duke Divinity School Review* volume 31, number 1 (Winter 1966), 20-38.

Rowe, Kenneth E. ed., *The Place of Wesley in the Christian Tradition* (Metuchen, N.J.: The Scarecrow Press, 1976).

Runyon, Theodore, ed., *Hope for The Church: Moltmann in Dialogue with Practical Theology* (Nashville: Abingdon, 1979).

_____, *Sanctification and Liberation* (Nashville: Abingdon, 1981).

_____, "What is Methodism's Theological Contribution Today?" in *Wesleyan Theology Today* (Nashville: Kingswood Books, 1985) 7-13.

_____, "A New Look at 'Experience,'" in *Drew Gateway* Fall 1987, 44-55.

Rutman, Darrett, B., ed., *The Great Awakening* (New York: John Wiley & Sons, 1970).

Ryle, Gilbert, *The Concept of Mind* (New York: Harper and Row, 1949).

_____, "Feelings" in *Philosophical Quarterly* 1 (1951), 193-205.

Saliers, Don E., *The Soul in Paraphrase: Prayer and the Religious Affections* (New York: The Seabury Press, 1980).

_____, *Worship and Spirituality* (Philadelphia: Westminster Press, 1984).

Sartre, Jean-Paul, *The Emotions: Outline of a Theory* (New York: Philosophical Library, 1948).

Schleiermacher, F.D.E., *The Christian Faith* (Philadelphia: Fortress, 1976)

Scroggs, Robin, "John Wesley as Biblical Scholar" in *Journal of Bible and Religion* volume XXVIII, number 4 (October 1969) 415-422.

Shimizu, Mitsuo, "Epistemology in the Theology of John Wesley" Ph.D. dissertation, Drew University, 1980.

Solomon, Robert and Calhoun, Cheshire, eds., *What is an Emotion?* (New York: Oxford University Press, 1984).

Southey, Robert, *The Life of Wesley and the Rise and Progress of Methodism* (London: Longmans, 1846) 2 volumes.

Stendahl, Krister, *Paul Among Jews and Gentiles* (Philadelphia: Fortress, 1976).

Stephen, Leslie, *History of English Thought in the Eighteenth Century* (New York: Putnam and Sons, 1902) 2 volumes.

_____, ed., *Dictionary of National Biography* (New York: Macmillan, 1896).

Stoeffler, F. Ernest, "Pietism, the Wesleys, and Methodist Beginnings in America" in *Continental Pietism and Early American Christianity* edited by Stoeffler (Grand Rapids: Eerdman's, 1976), 184-221.

Tuttle, Robert G., Jr., *John Wesley: His Life and Theology* (Grand Rapids: Zondervan Publishing House, 1978).

Wainwright, Geoffrey, review of John Deschner's book *Wesley's Christology* in *Perkins Journal* volume 39, number 2 (April 1986), 55-56.

Weidman, Judith, ed., *Christian Feminism* (San Francisco: Harper and Row, 1984).

West, Cornel, *Prophesy Deliverance!* (Philadelphia: Westminster Press, 1982).

White, James F., *John Wesley's Sunday Service* (Quarterly Review Reprint Series, 1984).

Williams, Colin W., *John Wesley's Theology Today* (New York: Abingdon, 1960).

Wood, A. Skevington, *The Burning Heart: John Wesley, Evangelist* (Exeter: Paternoster Press, 1967).

Wynkoop, Mildred Bangs, *A Theology of Love* (Kansas City: Beacon Hill Press, 1972).

Yandell, Keith E., *God, Man and Religion: Readings in Philosophy of Religion* (New York: McGraw Hill, 1973).

# INDEX

Abraham, William J., 20
abridgement(s), 24-25, **127-149**
action(s), relations to affections, 107, 167 (see also social nature of religion; works)
active/passive, 74
Adam, 53, 124
*Address to the Clergy*, 135
adultery, 36
aesthetics, 135, 137
affections and related terms, 2, 8, **46** (see also religious affections)
  and tempers, 51
  emphasized in O.T. *Notes*, **33-39**
agency, human, 66, **69-75**, 90
Ahlstrom, Sydney E., 151n
Albin, Thomas, x
Aldersgate, 105, 108, 109, 129, 151n
American Methodists, 20
anger, 37, 39, 88, 101, 102, 105, 122, 123, 155
Anglican heritage of Wesley, 9, 18, 152n
antinomianism, 126n
appetites, 54, 68, 90
Aquinas, St. Thomas, 13n, 17
Arminian, 31
Arnott, Felix R., 39n

*Articles of Religion*, 26, 109
Asbury Theological Seminary, ix
"Aspasia," 128
assurance, 90, **96n, 113-118**, 125n, 130
  degrees of, 117
atonement, 29, 104, 163-165
Augustine, ix, 13n, 95n, 125n
"Austin," (i.e., Augustine), 19
awe, 28, 35, 39, 87
Ayling, Stanley, 39n, 149n

Baker, Frank, x, 39n, 40n, 64n, 100, 125n, 139, 150n, 151n, 152n, 159
Baptism, 13n
Barr, James, 44
Barth, Karl, 164
Basil, 19
beatitudes, 174n (see also Sermon on the Mount)
beauty, 137, 153n
behavior, 162 (see also actions; works)
belief, 65n (see also faith)
Bence, Clarence L., 40n
Bengel, Johannes, 21, 24, 43, 64n
Benner, Forest T., 13n
Bernard of Clairvaux, 13n
Berntsen, John, 176n